J. H. (Joseph Hirst) Lupton

An Introduction to Latin Lyric Verse Composition

J. H. (Joseph Hirst) Lupton

An Introduction to Latin Lyric Verse Composition

ISBN/EAN: 9783744778893

Printed in Europe, USA, Canada, Australia, Japan

Cover: Foto ©Thomas Meinert / pixelio.de

More available books at **www.hansebooks.com**

TO

LATIN LYRIC VERSE COMPOSITION

BY

J. H. LUPTON, M.A.

SURMASTER OF ST. PAUL'S SCHOOL
AND FORMERLY FELLOW OF ST. JOHN'S COLLEGE, CAMBRIDGE

London
MACMILLAN AND CO.
AND NEW YORK
1888

All rights reserved

TO

THE REV. BENJAMIN HALL KENNEDY, D.D.
REGIUS PROFESSOR OF GREEK IN THE UNIVERSITY OF CAMBRIDGE

THIS LITTLE WORK IS

BY PERMISSION

MOST RESPECTFULLY DEDICATED

PREFACE

IN the previous *Introduction to Latin Elegiacs*, drawn up three years ago, I had chiefly in view the requirements of learners in my own class at St. Paul's. The present little work has been prepared with an eye to what such boys would be likely to require, when entering on the work of a higher form. My horizon has thus been a very limited one; and the only compensating advantage that can be looked for, is some reasonable familiarity with what lies within it. Whether, on this account, the book may be such as to prove serviceable to others, I do not hazard any opinion.

While reading—often with the liveliest admiration—the imitations of ancient poets by modern classical scholars, I have been increasingly struck with what seems to me a defect, pervading the work of all but the finished masters of the art,—a defect, not in the execution, but in the materials used. It is said to have been the judgment of Porson upon certain *Prolusiones*, that they contained "plenty of Horace and

Virgil, but nothing Horatian and nothing Virgilian." If I might presume to adapt this censure to the changed circumstances of our later time, I would say that with plenty of the Horatian and Virgilian spirit, there is too little of Horace and too little of Virgil. There is, at least,—and this is the more correct way of stating the matter—a not infrequent admixture of baser materials.

To confine myself to the subject specially in hand, Latin lyrics. If we remember the great sobriety of judgment Horace himself showed in introducing fresh words into his language,

> In verbis etiam tenuis cautusque serendis,—

skilful, indeed, to the last degree, in giving some new turn or shade of meaning to an existing word or phrase, but chary of devising new ones,—it is strange to see his modern imitators so venturesome. Without going so far as to say, that no Latin ode should go beyond the vocabulary of Horace, or no Latin elegiac beyond that of Ovid, it may be safely maintained that anything heterogeneous in such work is a blemish. Every term used, so far as possible, should be of contemporary style and character. To use Waltz's illustration from Horace himself, it should be, " signatum praesente nota." If, for example, we find freely admitted into modern Latin lyrics what are essentially prose words, or poetical compounds of a later date, or diminutive forms, we are justified in saying that, no matter how great the constructive skill, there are flaws in the materials.

A few specimens will best show what I mean. They are all taken from a collection of Latin lyrics, justly held in the highest esteem for the excellent work it contains, and one which, while fully conscious of my own temerity, I single out on that very account. A gleaning by no means thorough has brought away from it the following:—*Caelitus, stirpitus, praedocuit, procliatos, pronuntiavi, perlustrans, pervehi, transvehi, transigitur, jactitat, admurmurantem, praecaveant, repullulant, ingenitae, occidentalis, parasiticae, scrobs* and *deses* (as nominatives), *caritas, tarditas*. In one short piece alone are: *perpete, croletis, resarciuntur*.

It is proverbially hard to prove a negative; but I think none of these is used by an Augustan poet. They are strictly prose words; their use by the comic poets, in some instances, not affecting that character. If we could suppose an educated Roman of Horace's age reading an ode with such words in it, as the production of the poet of Venusia, the effect on his mind would surely have been akin to what is now produced by a peculiar species of American humour—enjoyable enough in its way—which turns on the introduction into poetry of words the most unpoetical. Such a result would be far indeed from what the writers intended.

The second class of words referred to is hardly less numerous. I mean that of compounds, and others, chiefly affected by the late poets. *Stelligeri, multisonus* and *penniger* all come together in one short ode, and are all, I believe, of the silver age. Other like creatures of the twilight, whether ante- or post-classical, are *terricolae, flavicomo, illicum,* and *praelibare.* The list might be considerably extended, if we added Lucretian words like *sursum,* or Catullian experiments like *imaginosa.*

Nor is the license less observable in the use of diminutives. Misled, apparently, by the influence of Catullus, or tempted by a seeming prettiness in harmony with modern taste, composers have had free recourse to a class of words that Horace appears to have deliberately avoided. The only diminutive he is shown to have coined for his Odes (if it was not already a technical term in use) is *parmula.* In his Satires and Epistles, which is quite a different matter, he has four or five more of his own invention. But in his imitators how great is the contrast! *Ocellus* recurs incessantly. So does *rivulus. Gemellos, lectulo, flosculi, paullulum, tenellulam, puellula, quantula* (after Juvenal), *aureola,* and the like, are members of the same interesting family.

I say nothing here of purely metrical licenses, such as the frequent leaving of a hiatus between the end of one line and the beginning of the next. This will be noticed more fully in the Introduction. If the remarks just made are warranted by the facts, they are enough to show the need of greater strictness in our imitations of Latin lyrics.[1]

The task of pointing out defects, real or supposed, is at best a thankless one, and exposes the adventurous person attempting it to many a crushing retort. Owning the force of these at once by anticipation, I will pass to the pleasanter duty of thanking those who have assisted me in my work.

To one indomitable scholar, whom more than two generations of students in this country have looked up to as a guide, I am allowed to acknowledge my long debt of gratitude in a dedication. To Lord Tennyson and to Mr. Swinburne my best acknowledgments are due for leave to make use of the short poems numbered XXXIX. and LII. respectively. Professor Nettleship has obliged me by the gift of two pieces of translation from his pen. Mrs. Shilleto has again kindly permitted me to insert a few copies of verse, the work of my former honoured tutor. When will a selection from his com-

---

[1] I may perhaps be allowed to say that two Assistant-masters of Eton, Mr. Wintle and Mr. Ainger, have in preparation a poetical Latin Dictionary, which will make it easier, in future, to discriminate the usage of words.

position—his Greek composition more especially—be given to the world? To four friends in particular my thanks are due, for help most generously afforded :—the Rev. C. Stanwell, formerly Fellow of St. John's; the Rev. Jackson Mason, Vicar of Settle; and Professors (now *emeriti*) James G. Lonsdale and F. A. Paley. In the companion book of Latin Renderings will be found a specific list of contributions.

St. Paul's School,
 September 1888.

CONTENTS

	PAGE
INTRODUCTION—	
§ 1. On Rhythm and Metre	xv
§ 2. On the Lyrical Metres of Horace	xxii
§ 3. Sapphic Metre	xxiv
§ 4. Alcaic Metre	xxix
§ 5. Asclepiad Metres	xxxv
§ 6. Pythiambic Metre	xli
§ 7. Systema Iambicum	xlii
§ 8. Iambic Senarius	xliv
§ 9. Synaphea in Horace	xliv
§ 10. Usage of Words in Horace	xlvii
§ 11. Miscellaneous Idioms	xlviii
Exercises in Sapphic Metre (I.-XX.)	1
,, Alcaic ,, (XXI.-XLVII.)	36
,, First Asclepiad Metre (XLVIII. XLIX.)	82
,, Second ,, ,, (L.-LII.)	86
,, Third ,, ,, (LIII.-LVI.)	92
,, Fourth ,, ,, (LVII.-LXV.)	99
,, Systema Pythiambicum (LXVI.-LXVII.)	111
,, Systema Iambicum (LXVIII.-LXIX.)	115
,, Trimetri Iambici (LXX.)	117
VOCABULARY	121
INDEX OF FIRST LINES	129

INTRODUCTION

§ 1. RHYTHM AND METRE

Rhythm is a term which can be applied to any movements recurring at regular intervals, as the ticking of a clock, the tramp of soldiers marching, the cantering of a horse. Such movements, as well as the sounds produced by them, are said to be rhythmical. If words are so grouped together as to produce similar effects, they are said to be in *metre*. The term *metrical* has, therefore, the same relation to language that *rhythmical* has to inarticulate sounds.

To understand the laws of metre, and the technical words employed, we can use no better illustration than that of dancing, especially such dancing as is described in Homer (*Il.* xviii. 567 *sqq.*), where one, standing in the midst, sings a song to the accompaniment of his lyre, while youths and maidens dance round him, joining in the song.[1] The same time must have been kept in the song, as in the accompaniment on the lyre, and in the dance. In what-

---

[1] For this illustration, and some remarks which follow, I am indebted to the *Leitfaden in der Rhythmik und Metrik der Classischen Sprachen*, of Dr. J. H. Heinrich Schmidt, 1869, pp. 19 *sqq.*

ever way, accordingly, we suppose the time to have been marked for the one, the other must have been susceptible of the same marks or divisions.

Now when a number of persons are keeping step together, either in marching or dancing, it is observed that the foot first raised from the ground is planted somewhat more firmly, or heavily, than the other. If recruits are being drilled in marching, to the call of "left, right! left, right!" we may notice the initial pause or balance on the right foot, followed by the decided planting of the left, which "marks the time." In like manner, in dancing, whichever foot leads off, we shall observe the momentary pause on the other, while that is uplifted, followed by its more marked and decided planting on the ground. If the dancers, as in Homer's *Linus*, or in a Greek chorus, are to sing as well, there must be a corresponding stress of the voice, recurring at fixed intervals, in time with the more distinctly-marked tread of the feet. Hence it has come about that terms strictly applicable to marching or dancing have been used to distinguish metre. The planting of the foot with a firm, well-marked tread, was called *thesis*. Its raising, while the less distinctly-marked tread was made by the other, was called *arsis*. And these terms have been applied (by modern writers, however, in just the converse sense) to the alternations of stress and lightness in metrical feet. In fact, the very term *foot*, used to designate the component parts of a metre, bears witness to the close connection once existing between the song and the dance.

The learner will find it a useful exercise to recite aloud, or sing to any suitable air, passages in well-marked metre like the following; and try to hear mentally, at the same time, the sound of feet marching or dancing to the tune. If he can be his own *choreutes*, so much the better.[1]

> "Rally round the flag, boys,
>   Give it to the breeze!
> That's the banner *we* love
>   On the land and seas.
> Let our colours fly, boys,
>   Guard them day and night!
> For victory is liberty,
>   And God will bless the right."

> "Merrily, merrily shall I live now
> Under the blossom that hangs on the bough."

> "We sigh for our country, we mourn for our dead;
> For them now our last drop of blood we will shed:
> Our cause is the right one, our foe's in the wrong,
> Then gladly we'll sing as we're marching along."

In the first of these extracts, the ear will catch four beats or *ictuses* in each of the longer lines, and three in each of the other. Moreover, the first and third beats are stronger and more marked than the second and fourth. If we imagine soldiers starting to march to the sound of these lines, sung to a musical accompaniment, the first, or strong step, made with the left foot, will coincide with the first syllable in "Rally"; the second, or less strongly-marked one, with the right, will coincide with "round," and so on.

---

[1] "With regard to the strictly lyrical parts of poetry ... I have no hesitation in saying, that the only proper way to obtain a full perception of their rhythmical beauty is to sing or chant them to any extemporised melody; which would be much more readily done were not music so unworthily neglected in our higher schools."—Professor Blackie, *On the Pronunciation of Greek*, 1852, p. 64. The defect Professor Blackie complains of has been largely supplied since he wrote.

In the seventh line, an initial syllable, "for," precedes the strong beat on the first syllable of "victory." This answers to the *anacrusis* before spoken of, and represents the pause or lighter tread on the right foot, before the more distinctly-marked tread of the left. It will be noticed that such a light syllable has really to be allowed for, in the time, at the end of each of the shorter lines. Otherwise the strong beat would come twice in succession. The second line, for instance, is timed as if it really were: "Give it to the breezes." In music, the place of the syllable thus allowed for would be denoted by a *rest* of the proper duration.

Comparing the second and third extracts, we observe that they differ only in the fact that the initial syllable, or *anacrusis*, is present in the latter, absent in the former. If the first line of the couplet from the *Tempest* began with "Oh," the metre would be the same in both. Being in triple time, these lines could be sung to certain kinds of dance music. The first syllable in "merrily" would answer to the strong tread of the left foot stepping out, followed by two lighter steps of the right and left alternately: the syllables of the second "merrily" would answer to a like succession of movements, beginning with the right foot; and so on. To make the metre of the words correspond exactly to the movement of the feet, it is obvious that two short syllables must be supplied, or equivalent time allowed for them, at the end of each line.

This illustration may help to make clearer what is meant by metrical *ictus*, or stress, and also by the terms *thesis* and *arsis*, as rightly employed by the old Greek musicians.

At this point comes in the difficulty, how to reconcile the claims of the *ictus* with those of accent and quantity. This may be partly cleared up by observing that we do not now use the word *accent* in the classical sense. In modern parlance, *accent* is much the same as stress or emphasis. If we say that the first syllable of *honest* bears the accent, we merely mean that we lay a greater stress on that syllable in pronouncing it. We do not mean that it is uttered at a higher pitch, or takes a longer time to articulate, than the second. But the derivation of the word *accent* (*ad*, *cantus*) shows that it originally had reference to singing. Accentual marks were called in Greek *prosodiae*, with the same meaning. We lose sight of the fact that in our ordinary speech the syllables of words are enunciated, not only with varying degrees of force, but in higher or lower tones. Sometimes, perhaps generally, the higher pitch will coincide with the greater stress, but this is by no means always the case. Listen to a Frenchman, saying, in answer to a question, "pas un mot." The second syllable will always be (at least, in my experience) both higher in pitch and more emphasised than the others. But listen to the question, in English, "is it credible?" The first syllable of "credible," will be lower in pitch, though at the same time more emphasised, than the rest. An English child, calling out "Henry!" would probably sing the notes F and C; while a German child, crying "Heinrich" would reverse the scale. Yet both would emphasise the first syllable. More examples are needless to show that *accent*, in the proper sense, and *ictus*, or stress, can exist in the same word independently of each other. The same holds good with respect to *quantity*,—the length of time taken in enunciating a syllable, or during which a vowel sound is prolonged. Take for instance the word *entrance*. It cannot be said that the duration of the second syllable in point of time is less than that of the first, which bears the accent. The word "Westminster" is pronounced with the accent (in its modern sense of *ictus*, or stress) sometimes on the first, sometimes on the second. If, as may be sometimes heard at a railway station, it is pronounced with the stress on the first, with a slight elevation of voice on the second, and with all three syllables equal in point of duration, we have a good example of *ictus*, accent, and quantity all coexisting independently in one word.

The difficulty, however, is not yet cleared up, how far, in singing, or metrical composition, accent (in its proper sense) yielded to *ictus*, or became identified with it. In Latin there are no accentual marks to guide us. The main rules of accentuation for that language are very simple. Subject to some few exceptions, which need not here be noticed, every dissyllable has the accent on its penult, independently of the quantity of either syllable, and every word of three or more syllables has the accent on the penult, if it be long; on the antepenult, if it be short. Originally the accents were three, as in Greek; the acute, as in *bónos, dóminos,* and the circumflex, as in *verberáre*. The grave accent was understood on all syllables not bearing either of these. But by the end of the twelfth century the distinction between the acute and circumflex accent ceased to be recognised;[1] so that practically we have only one accent, the acute, to consider in Latin words. That the accented syllable also bore the *ictus;* or, in other words,

---

[1] *Traité élémentaire d'accentuation Latine*, par l'Abbé Viot, 1888, p. 8. See also King and Cookson's *Sounds and Inflexions*, 1888, p. 284.

that a syllable in Latin was accentuated in the modern sense; seems to have been the case in many instances.[1] But if the two things, accent and *ictus*, are to be considered as always identical in Latin, I am at a loss how to explain the circumstance, that the metrical ictus by no means always coincides with the verbal accent. "The ancients," in fact, as is observed by one well entitled to speak on such a subject, "made it a special point that their verses should not *scan themselves*"—in other words, that *ictus* and accent should not coincide—"and every form of line which did so they held bad on that account."[2] Such a fourth line of an alcaic, for instance, as *frangere corpora nescit aevum*, though correct as far as the scansion goes, would be intolerable.

Whatever be the solution of the difficulty about the non-accordance of the metrical and verbal *ictus* (supposing that *accent* in Latin words implied stress, and not elevation of voice only), the learner should carefully notice where a Roman poet requires them to agree. Thus in the Pherecratian line of Horace, *nigris aequora ventis*, the first syllable must always be accented. In quadrisyllables like *interfusa, insignemque*, which Horace admits, there is a secondary accent on the first, as well as the stronger on the third. Hence such a line as *ridebant pueriles* would be inadmissible, from the accent coming on the second syllable.

---

[1] This is assumed in the derivations of *optumus, surgere*, etc., in King and Cookson (*ib.*) The Abbé Viot also speaks of "la force et l'élévation de la voix sur les syllabes accentuées," as if they were one and the same thing.

[2] *Literary Remains of Charles Stuart Calverley*, 1885, p. 174.

§ 2. THE LYRICAL METRES OF HORACE

Bearing in mind that lyrical odes, or *carmina* (as Horace himself calls them) are properly odes to be sung to the accompaniment of a lyre, we proceed to examine the metres which he used in the composition of his pieces. In an elementary treatise like the present, it will be impossible to follow him through the whole of his wide range. Little else will accordingly be studied than the *Sapphic*, the *Alcaic*, and the several varieties of the *Asclepiad* metre; being those which Horace himself adopted most frequently.

It will be found of service, at the outset, to notice the chronological order of the Books of the Odes, as we may thus learn how the poet's taste altered as time went on, and what we may suppose him to have preferred, as bearing the sanction of his riper judgment.

Without entering into any minute discussion of controverted questions, it may be said that Horace did not begin his Odes till he had finished the two books of Satires and the Epodes. The earliest ode that can be certainly dated is i. 37, written on the death of Cleopatra in the autumn of B.C. 30.[1] The latest ode in point of time in the first three Books is thought to be i. 12, referring to the death of Marcellus in the autumn of B.C. 23. Regarding the first three Books, then, as a whole, we may say that its contents were written at various times between B.C. 30 and B.C. 23 (between the years 35 and 42 of the poet's own life), and published soon after the latter date. An interval of some

---

[1] See Hirschfelder's edition of Orelli's *Horace*, 1885, i. p. xxxviii, and Wickham's *Horace*, 1877, p. 2.

length intervened before the publication of the fourth Book. The sixth Ode in it, and the *Carmen Saeculare* must be assigned to B.C. 17; while several Odes refer to the return of Augustus in B.C. 13. We may conclude, therefore, that the fourth Book was not published till at least ten years after the first three, and that its composition occupied the years 48-52 of his own life. Horace died B.C. 8, when he had nearly completed his fifty-seventh year.

It will thus be seen that there is a difference in the weight of authority to be assigned to quotations from Horace, according to the period at which they were written. When appealed to as standards of correctness, or elegance, it is not only insufficient to allege a passage from the Epodes, for example, as authority in an imitation of the Odes; but what is allowed in the later books of the Odes must be discriminated from what is allowed in the earlier ones. The Epodes,[1] or *iambi*, as Horace calls them, invectives after the style of Archilochus, naturally go with his other early compositions, the Satires. They occupy somewhat the same place in his literary career as the *English Bards and Scotch Reviewers* holds in that of Lord Byron. The Odes must be the only pattern of style and diction for professed imitations of Horace's lyrical poems; and they must be so, to some degree, with an ascending value according to the sequence of the Books. If in the Fourth Book and the *Carmen Saeculare* we find an increasing preference of the caesura after the sixth syllable in the Sapphic verse, we shall think less of the imitations of Statius (*Silv.* iv. 7) and Prudentius, where the caesura after the fifth is observed

[1] For the meaning of the term *Epode*, see Wickham, as above, p. 325.

without any variation. We shall also be more jealous of admitting a short syllable at the beginning of an Alcaic line, when we remark that there is not a single instance of it in the Fourth Book. Further details under this head may, however, be best reserved for the discussion of the metres one by one.

§ 3. SAPPHIC METRE[1]

The Sapphic, Alcaic and Asclepiad metres, which include among them the great majority of all composed by Horace, are known by the general name of *logaœdic*, because the intermixture of trochees and dactyls, of which they consist, was supposed to give them a character intermediate between the restrained flow of ordinary speech (*logos*) and the freer tide of song (*aoide*). There is this external peculiarity common to them all, that, with one exception, the number of lines in each ode is a multiple of four. Hence Meineke, and most scholars after him, would arrange all the Odes of Horace in *strophes*, or stanzas, of four lines each, and would reduce the solitary offender (iv. 8) at all costs to subjection.[2] The learner, at any rate, must be careful so to arrange his rendering of a passage into lyrics, as to produce an exact number of four-line stanzas.

---

[1] For many remarks in this and the following sections I am indebted to Riemann's French translation of the *Metres lyriques d'Horace* par H. Schiller, 1883 ; Lucian Müller's *Metrik der Griechen und Römer*, 1885 ; the same writer's Prolegomena to the Teubner *Horace*, 1887 ; Waltz's *Des Variations de la Langue et de la Métrique d'Horace*, 1881 ; Tate's *Horatius Restitutus;* and Verrall's *Studies . . . in the Odes of Horace*, 1884.

[2] Hirschfelder leaves it as it is.

In beginning with the Sapphic metre, I am following the usual practice in English schools, though I do not myself think it so easy to write as some forms of the Asclepiad. The name is derived from the poetess of Lesbos (circ. B.C. 600). Her splendid ode to Aphrodite, and some fragments, suffice to show the construction of the metre in her hands, and, by comparison, the changes made in it by Horace. The chief points which distinguish the Greek Sapphic are these three:—(1) A free use of the trochee as the second foot; (2) a greater variety in the caesura; (3) a union of the third and fourth lines (as they were afterwards regarded) in one. In the few Sapphic lines of Catullus which remain, we see this freedom but little curtailed:—

"Gallicum Rhenum horribilem insulam ultimosque Britannos."
"Qui sedens aduersus identidem te
Spectat et audit."
"Otium, Catulle, tibi molestum est."

Horace put a strict restraint on this variety, though relaxing somewhat in his later compositions. For the optional trochee in the second foot he invariably substituted a spondee. Of the various caesuras, he admitted only two: that at the end of the fifth syllable, as in

Serus in caelum | redeas, diuque   (A.)

and that at the end of the sixth, as in

Mercuri, facunde | nepos Atlantis.   (B.)

And, lastly, he went beyond Catullus in disconnecting the latter part of the long third line from the rest, so as to justify the view afterwards taken of it as a separate fourth line.

With regard to the caesura, it must be observed that while the form marked (A) is far commoner in Horace than (B), 567 lines out of 615 having the former,[1] and only 48 the latter; yet of these 48 a great majority are found in the later odes. The first and second books have only 7 between them; the third not a single example; while the fourth book has 22, and the *Carmen Saeculare* (of 76 lines) has 19. It would thus seem that Horace, in his maturer judgment, was inclined to admit this particular caesura more freely. In the *Carmen Saeculare* some special effects were probably aimed at.

How far the short fourth line (called a *versus Adonius*, from the refrain of Greek dirges on Adonis) should be regarded as disconnected by Horace from the third, is a disputed point. In three instances he favours the theory of their continuity by dividing a word between them:—

> Labitur ripa Iove non probante u-
>   xorius amnis (i. 2. 19)
> Thracio bacchante magis sub inter-
>   lunia vento (i. 25. 11)
> Grosphe, non gemmis neque purpura ve-
>   nale nec auro (ii. 16. 7).

But the non-elision between the third and fourth lines in

> Neve te nostris vitiis iniquum
>   Ocior aura (i. 2. 47)
> Nec Iubae tellus generat, leonum
>   Arida nutrix (i. 22. 15)

as well as the *collision*, or contact of vowels not usually elided, in

---

[1] The computation is Schiller's.

> Vnde vocalem temere insecutae
> Orphea silvae (i. 12. 7)
> Et minax, cum sic voluere, ponto
> Vnda recumbit (i. 12. 31)

are held to bear out the view commonly taken. . It should be noticed, however, how very few these examples are, and that one of them at least (i. 12. 7) is open to suspicion. When it is added that, out of the 850 Sapphic lines of Horace there can only be produced some seven cases of non-elision of a short vowel or *-um* at the end of a line, before a vowel at the beginning of the next [1] (i. 12. 40; i. 32. 12; ii. 6. 8; ii. 8. 8; ii. 16. 28; iii. 27. 36; iv. 11. 12), and that most of these can be explained by a pause in the sense, the learner will see good reason to avoid, as far as possible, any such hiatus between his own lines. But more will be said on this subject in a following section on *synaphea*.

It may be further noticed that a long syllable is preferable to a short one at the end of any Sapphic line. The proportion is about two to one for the long lines, and three to two for the short Adonic. The table of feet will thus be as follows:—

$$1, 2, 3, \quad -\cup\; \stackrel{\prime}{-}\; -\; \stackrel{\prime}{-} \mid \cup\cup\; \stackrel{\prime}{}\; \cup\; \stackrel{\prime}{-}\; \stackrel{\smile}{-}$$
$$4, \quad \stackrel{\prime}{-}\; \cup\cup\; \stackrel{\prime}{-}\; \stackrel{\smile}{-}$$

With the caesura after the sixth syllable, the scheme for the first three lines will be—

$$\stackrel{\prime}{-}\; \cup\; \stackrel{\prime}{-}\; -\; \stackrel{\prime}{-}\; \cup \mid \cup\; \stackrel{\prime}{-}\; \cup\; \stackrel{\prime}{-}\; \cup$$

How the feet should be classified in the verse itself is a point on which scholars are not agreed. It is usually described as consisting of trochees and dactyls. Schiller

---

[1] The calculation is Dr. Verrall's, *ubi sup.*, p. 180.

speaks, somewhat fancifully, of "le dactyle, qui, dans chacun des trois premiers vers, interrompt par son allure plus rapide la marche tranquille et mesurée des trochées." Others, however, as the late Professor Key, argue strongly in favour of the central part of the verse, the nucleus, as it were, being a choriambus ($-\smile\smile-$), to which a trochaic dipodia (Horace displacing the second trochee by a spondee) is prefixed, and an iambic dipodia (wanting one syllable) is subjoined. This missing syllable at the end would answer to the rest at the end of an incomplete bar of music.

The point in dispute is not of so much practical concern to the learner as is a right method of reciting the verse aloud. The metrical ictus will be the same, or nearly so, whether the middle syllables are regarded as forming a dactyl, followed by a trochee, or a choriambus. But between the two methods of reciting, most in use, there is a great difference of principle. The one preserves the verbal accent, to the neglect of the metrical ictus; the other does just the reverse. According to the one method, for instances, the following lines would be read :—

> Iam satis terris nivis átque dirae
> Grándinis misit pater et rubénte, etc.

According to the other:

> Iam satis terris nivis átque dirae
> Grándinis misit pater et rubénte, etc.

The beginning and end of the line receives nearly the same stress in each system, but a great difference is felt in the treatment of the central part, especially as regards the syllable before the strong cæsura. And the first of the two seems to fail when tried by three tests :—(1) It is not adapted to the trochaic, or sixth-syllable caesura, as in

> Mercuri, facunde nepos Atlantis,

(2) it does not accord with the strong ictus required for the scansion of ii. 6. 14,

> Angulus ridet | ubi non Hymetto ;

and (3) it does not suit the Alcaic line, which is plainly the same as the Sapphic, with a syllable removed from the end to the beginning of the verse. For example, by such a change,

> Méntis ét curás laqueáta círcum

will become

> Cúm méntis ét curás laqueáta cír-

which, excepting for the caesura, is an Alcaic line.

It may be noticed, in concluding this section, that the Sapphic metre was regarded as specially fitted for prayers and invocations of the Gods. Thus the great ode of Sappho herself, in this metre, was a prayer to Aphrodite. Horace chose it for his *Carmen Saeculare*. In it he invokes Quirinus, Mercury, and so on. At the same time he does not confine the metre to this purpose, but occasionally writes lighter pieces in it, as i. 38, ii. 4.

§ 4. ALCAIC METRE

As far as mere difficulty is concerned, this metre might well have been postponed to the last, as most persons will agree that it is the hardest to write of all the commoner metres of Horace. It is, however, his favourite metre : no fewer than thirty-seven Odes, or about one-third of all his lyrics, being composed in it. And it deserves this preference from its own merits, being of a grand and stately movement, especially fitted for martial or patriotic subjects. It should be one of the first cares of the learner to commit to memory the noble collection of Alcaic Odes in the Third Book.

The metre takes its name from Alcaeus, of Lesbos, a contemporary of Sappho. We have only fragments of his odes remaining; but enough, as in the case of Sappho also, to show what changes or restrictions Horace introduced. These changes were mainly the following:—

(1) While Alcaeus has the first syllable, or anacrusis, in the first, second, and third lines, short or long indifferently, Horace made it almost invariably long. Out of 634 such lines, 17 only begin with a short syllable; and of these, 8 are in the first Book, 4 in the second, 5 in the third, while in the fourth there is not a single instance. The shortening of the first syllable is also seldomer found in the third line, than in the first or second.[1]

(2) The second trochee in lines 1-3, freely admitted by Alcaeus, is replaced, almost without exception, by a spondee in Horace. There is, however, the exception, supported by all the MSS., of iii. 5. 17, "Si non periret immiserabilis," etc.

(3) The caesura, especially in the third line, was made by Horace much more definite and limited. What is meant will be best shown presently by a few examples.

---

[1] Tennyson has an example of the short syllable:—
"Me rather all that bowery loneliness,
 The brooks of Eden mazily murmuring."

The scale of feet is as follows:—

1. $\stackrel{\smile}{-} - \smile - \ \cdots\ \cdot\ \smile\smile - \smile \stackrel{\smile}{-}$
2. $\stackrel{\smile}{-} - \smile - - \mid\ \cdot\ \smile\smile\ \ \smile\ \stackrel{\smile}{\smile}$
3. $\stackrel{\smile}{-} \ \smile\ -\ -\ -\ \smile\ \ \ \stackrel{\smile}{-}$
4. $-\smile\smile - \smile\smile - \smile\ \cdot\ \stackrel{\smile}{-}$

It becomes clear, from an inspection of the above, that the metre is formed of the same elements as the Sapphic. In the first two lines, if we take off the first syllable, as an anacrusis, and place it at the end, we have a Sapphic line. The third and fourth lines are expansions of the first and second halves of the preceding lines; the third adding a trochaic dipodia to the first half, and the fourth to the second half, respectively. Compare, for example, the following pairs of first and third lines, and second and fourth, when set together.

{ Portare fustes | sol ubi montium
{ Versare glebas | et severae.
Parvosque natos { ut capitis minor
{ Qua tumidus rigat arva Nilus.

The caesura in the first and second lines is almost always after the fifth syllable, that is (if we regard the first syllable as an anacrusis) at the end of the trochaic dipodia. The only exceptions are

Mentemque lymphatam Mareotico (i. 37. 14)
Spectandus in certamine Martio (iv. 14. 17)
Hostile aratrum exercitus insolens (i. 16. 21)
Antehac nefas depromere Caecubum (i. 37. 5)
Utrumque nostrum incredibili modo (ii. 17. 21).

Of these, the last three are only partial violations of the rule, owing to the word in which the caesura falls being compounded with a preposition. The first two cannot be got over.[1] Sometimes (in about twenty cases) there is a quasi-caesura, owing to elision, as in

> Regum timendorum in proprios greges (iii. 1. 5).

The apparent irregularity in the following is to be got over by giving a consonantal force to the letter *i* :—

> Vos lene consilium et datis, et dato iii. 4. 41)
> Hinc omne principium, huc refer exitum (iii. 6. 6).

When we come to the third line, it is less easy to fix on one definite place for the caesura. Horace admits several varieties of rhythm, while others he seems carefully to exclude. The only course, therefore, is to study his various forms of the third line, and select those which he employs most often.

If we were guided by the theory that the third line is an expansion of the first half of the first or second, we might expect to find the caesura in the same place as it occupies there. And this is sometimes the case, as in

> Non Liber aeque, non acuta (i. 16. 7).

But this is by no means the favourite pattern. Indeed, if a third line begins in such a way that its first half might stand as the first half of the previous line, its ending has to be very skilfully managed for it to be admissible at all.

Taking, then, the forms of the third line most often found, in the order of their frequency, we have the following :[2]

---

[1] Hirschfelder prints them without any attempt at alteration. Müller obelises the lines. Schiller proposes, in the first line, *lymphatam a.*

[2] I have here availed myself of the results worked out by Tate, in his *Horatius Restitutus,* p. 191.

A. Defendit | aestatem | capellis (i. 17. 3)
B. Visam | pharetratos | Gelonos (iii. 4. 35)
C. Declive | contempleris | arvum (iii. 29. 7)
D. Portus | Alexandrea | supplex (iv. 14. 35)
E. Non | erubescendis | adurit (i. 27. 15)
F. Deproeliantes | nec | cupressi (i. 9. 11).

Of these (A) is far the commonest, representing nearly half the entire number of third lines. Beginners may perhaps remember it by the words "September, October, November." On the other hand, that marked (C) is one which Horace appears to have shown a growing preference for in his later lyrics, being found much oftener in the third and fourth books than in the first and second. It must be noted that while, for convenience of remembering, lines containing only three words each have been chosen as examples, such lines are in reality few in number. So long as the caesuras are observed, the single intervening words may be replaced by a combination of two or more words *bearing the same accent.* Thus we may have, under the several headings—

A. In párte | regnánto | beáti
   Per dámna, | per caédes | ab ípso
B. Súcos | et adscríbi | quiétis
   Téndens | Venafrános | in ágros
C. Devóta | non exstínxit | árbor
   Hic clásse | formidátus | ílle
D. Nóstros | et adiecísse | praédam
   Lúdo | fatigatúmque | sómno
E. Núnc | in reluctántes | dracónes
   Dúlcem | elaborábunt | sopórem
F. Vix illigátum | té | trifórmi
   Portáre véntis | quis | sub Árcto

besides other varieties. For a time, at least, the learner will do well to confine himself to the first three of these types.

Some of those found in Horace are not easy to copy, from the length or other peculiarity of the words. Such are

   Deprocliantes, nec cupressi (i. 9. 11)
   Denominatos, et nepotum (iii. 17. 3).

Others are either very rarely used by him, or offend the ear by their want of harmony. Such are

   Hunc Lesbio sacraro plectro (i. 26. 11)
   Depone sub lauru mea, nec ii. 7. 19.

It may be laid down, as a general rule, that the third line should neither begin nor end with a quadrisyllable, or with two dissyllables. Lines of the form of

   Pronos relabi posse rivos (i. 29. 11)
   Nodo coerces viperino (ii. 19. 19),

though found eleven times in all in the first and second books, are excluded from the third and fourth.

The fourth line admits of about the same number of varieties as the third, but the beginner will not be in the same danger of going wrong. His chief care must be not to make the cæsuras coincide with the divisions of feet. As Calverley remarks, Tennyson's line

   "Calm as a | wanderer | out in | ocean"

would be exactly represented, in form, by

   Sol ut in | aere | lucet | alto.

But the Latin line would be bad, as the fourth of an Alcaic stanza. Grouping those used by Horace in order of frequency, as before, we have—

   A. Composita | repetantur | hora (i. 9. 20)
   B. Sardiniae segetes | feraces (i. 31. 4).

C. Gaudia | luminibus | remotis (iii. 6. 28)
D. Roma ferox | dare | iura | Medis (iii. 3. 44)
E. Levia | personuere saxa (i. 17. 12)
F. Cuncta | supercilio | moventis (iii. 1. 8).

Of these (A) is the most numerous, while (D) appears to have grown in favour with Horace, being much oftener found in his later books than in the earlier. It will not be necessary to furnish the learner with examples of the way in which any of the long words in the above list can be replaced by combinations of shorter ones. He will be able to form such combinations for himself, by the help of the previous table.

It should be added that the final syllable in each Alcaic line is long by preference. In the first and second lines, out of 634 in all, 319 are long and 315 short; so that the proportion is nearly equal. But in the third lines, out of half the above total, 205 are long, 112 short; and in the same number of fourth lines 209 are long, 108 short.

§ 5. Asclepiad Metres

The general name of Asclepiad is given to five systems employed by Horace, being all combinations, in varying forms, of two simple lines, the Glyconic and Pherecratian. As will be readily conjectured, these titles are given to them from the names of their supposed inventors, or of those first known to use them. Asclepiades is said to have lived about the time of Sappho and Alcaeus. Of Glycon nothing survives but three solitary lines, preserved by Hephaestion. Pherecrates is better known. He was but little senior to Aristophanes, and in some verses still extant claims the invention of the metre named after him.

The germ, or nucleus, of them all alike is the choriambus ($-\ \smile\smile\ -$). If this is preceded by a trochee (for which Horace uses a spondee), and followed by an iambus, the line is a Glyconic—

$$-\ -\ |\ -\ \smile\smile\ -\ |\ \smile\ \breve{\ }$$
Audax | Iapeti | genus.

If, instead of the final iambus (or pyrrhic, $\smile\smile$), the choriambus is followed by a long syllable, the line is a Pherecratian:—

$$-\ -\ |\ -\ \smile\smile\ -\ |\ -$$
Nigris | aequora ven | tis.

This, to the eye, is identical with one form of the ending of an hexameter line; and it is of course possible to read it as such. But let any one recite, with proper intonation, hexameter lines ending in an apparent Pherecratian, as

Ille graves urbes, hic | durae limen amatae
Nec mora, venit amor, non | umbras nocte silentes,

and he will be conscious of the difference. In the true Pherecratian there is a more sustained pause on the last syllable but one—

Grato Pyrrha sub antro,

which makes the time not differ perceptibly from that of the Glyconic—

Felices ter et amplius.

Agreeably with this, while the Glyconic may end in two short syllables ($\smile\smile$ instead of $\smile -$), as in

Vestra motus aget prece,

the last syllable of the Pherecratian is invariably long in Horace. By some writers, indeed, the two species are classed under one common name, Glyconic.

Horace has no ode in either of these measures alone; but when variously combined and expanded they form the five Asclepiad metres. The first[1] Asclepiad is simply a Glyconic with the choriambus doubled. The second is formed by an alternation of the Glyconic and first Asclepiad. The third is in four-line stanzas, consisting of three first Asclepiads, followed by a Glyconic. The fourth in like manner consists of two first Asclepiads, a Pherecratian, and a Glyconic. The fifth is the same as the first, with the choriambus tripled, instead of doubled. Of this last variety (being monotonous, and only three times used by Horace), no specimen is given in the following Exercises. It will be convenient to tabulate the four previous ones together.

First Asclepiad

$$- - - \cup \cup - \mid - \cup \cup - \cup \breve{}$$
Maecenas atavis | edite regibus.

(i. 1.)

Second Asclepiad

$$- - - \cup \cup - \cup -$$
$$- - - \cup \cup - \mid - \cup \cup - \cup \breve{}$$
Sic te diva potens Cypri
Sic fratres Helenae | lucida sidera.

(i. 3.)

---

[1] In numbering them I have followed the order of Schiller and Hirschfelder. Wickham (p. 382) makes what is above called the fifth, to be the second Asclepiad.

Third Asclepiad

```
— — — ᴜ ᴜ — | — ᴜ ᴜ — ᴜ ˇ̄
— — — ᴜ ᴜ — | — ᴜ ᴜ — ᴜ ˇ̄
— — — ᴜ ᴜ — | — ᴜ ᴜ — ᴜ ˇ̄
        — — ᴜ ᴜ — ᴜ
```

Scriberis Vario   fortis et hostium
Victor, Maeonii   carminis aliti,
Quam rem cumque ferox | navibus aut equis
        Miles te duce gesserit.

                                     (i. 6.)

Fourth Asclepiad

```
— — — ᴜ ᴜ — | — ᴜ ᴜ — ᴜ ˇ̄
— — — ᴜ ᴜ — | — ᴜ ᴜ — ᴜ ˇ̄
— —     — ᴜ ᴜ — —
— —     — ᴜ ᴜ — ᴜ —
```

Quis multa gracilis | te puer in rosa
Perfusus liquidis | urget odoribus
        Grato, Pyrrha, sub antro?
        Cui flavam religas comam.

                                     (i. 5.)

The Glyconic and Pherecratian, as they appear in Greek (for instance in choral odes and among the pieces assigned to Anacreon) are much less severely constructed than by Horace. They often begin with a trochee, and this trochee, as well as the second (or end of the choriambus) may be resolved, as in Eur. *Phœn.* 227, while the last syllable of the Pherecratian may be short (*ib.* 213). Catullus, in his Nuptial Ode (*Carm.* lxi.), which is arranged in stanzas of four Glyconics, followed by a Pherecratian, imitates the Greek, in beginning with a trochee. But he has in one line (v. 25) a license all his own, in substituting a spondee for the dactylic beginning of the choriambus: "nutriunt umore."

Horace allows no such variations. As he braced up the lax trochee in the second foot of the Sapphic to a spondee, so he makes a spondee, almost invariably, to begin his Asclepiad lines. The only exceptions are in two contested lines of a single Ode (i. 15. 24, 36)—

> Teucĕr, et Sthenelus sciens
> Ignīs Iliacas domos.[1]

If genuine, the Greek construction of the verse may have been thought to harmonise with the names introduced.

The cæsura in the First Asclepiad, and in the same line where introduced in the others, is always after the first choriambus—

> Cressa ne careat | pulchra dies nota.

The exceptions are only such as prove the rule. In ii. 12. 25 we have

> Nec flagrantia de | torquet ad oscula,

where the preposition takes the cæsura, as was noticed before in the case of i. 37. 5; and in iv. 8. 17,

> Non incendia Car | thaginis inpiae :

of which it is sufficient to say that it occurs in the Ode already referred to as being the only example of an irregular number of lines. The MSS. however give no alternative for Carthaginis; and even Hermann, who rewrote the

---

[1] L. Müller, and others, alter both passages, by reading *te* for *et* in the first line, and *Pergameas*, for *Iliacas*, in the second. The latter alteration has no MS. authority.

Ode, left it undisturbed. The caesura comes after a monosyllable oftener than might have been expected, as in

> Digne scripserit, aut | pulvere Troico (i. 6. 14)
> Atqui non ego te | tigris ut aspera (i. 23. 9)
> Languescit mihi, nec | pinguia Gallicis (iii. 16. 35).

Generally, however, the monosyllable will be found to be closely connected with what precedes, and sometimes so by elision, as in

> O et praesidium et | dulce decus meum (i. 1. 2)
> Nos, Agrippa, neque haec | dicere nec gravem (i. 6. 5).

The caesura is also occasionally found with an elision, as in

> Vitabis strepitumque | et celerem sequi (i. 15. 18)
> Hic bellum lacrimosum | hic miseram famem (i. 21. 13).

In the short third line, or Pherecratian, of the fourth Asclepiad, there must be no elision. The materials are not, indeed, abundant for constructing a rule, as there are only 35 lines of this pattern in Horace. But in none of these is there any elision. The first and last syllables must be always long, and the first accented. In only one instance is a monosyllable found at the end—

> Portum, nonne vides, ut (i. 14. 3).

In the fourth, or Glyconic, line somewhat more freedom is allowed. Elisions are allowed, as in

> Ludisque et bibis impudens (iv. 13. 1)
> Dilapsam in cineres facem (iv. 13. 28)
> Nil mortalibus arduist (i. 3. 37).

The last syllable may also be short. The fourth line, in fact, stands to the third in much the same relation as the last of an Alcaic stanza does to the one before it. In each case the resolution of a long vowel makes the difference—

> Dēprōme quadrimum Sabina }
> Dēprĭme quadrivium Sabina. }
> Suspendisse potenti }
> Suspendisse potentĭbŭs. }

The delicate shades of lightness in the various forms of the Asclepiad metre, rising from the almost Alcaic dignity of the third ("Scriberis Vario," etc.) to the playful badinage of the fourth ("Quis multa gracilis," etc.), make it very suitable for pieces of a thoughtful, reflective cast, as well as for lighter *jeux d'esprit*. About the second, in particular ("Quem tu, Melpomene, semel," etc.), there is a certain plaintive cast, suiting it for reminiscences of past life, and the like, such as Macaulay's fine lines, beginning—

> "The day of tumult, strife, defeat, was o'er."

§ 6. Pythiambic Metre

The name of this metre (*Pythius, iambus*) is intended to denote the combination in it of a dactylic hexameter (in which the Pytho, or priestess of Apollo at Delphi, gave her responses) and an iambic line. For our present purpose, we are only concerned with what is known as the First Pythiambic, where the metre consists of hexameters and iambic dimeters alternately. Of this there are only two specimens in Horace, *Epod.* xiv. and xv. Each of these two consists of an exact multiple of four lines: but that this is accidental is pretty clear from the next (*Epod.* xvi. in second Pythiambic metre), which has 66 lines. The composition of the hexameters calls for no particular remark, except that the first of all has what, by other standards, would be called an inelegant caesura

> Mollis inertia cur | tantam diffuderit imis ;

a verse, as Waltz points out, like that in *Od.* iv. 7. 7,

> Immortalia ne | speres, monet annus et almum.

In the iambic dimeters, the spondee is freely admitted in the first and third places. In the last line of all, there is a dactyl in the first place—

> Ast ego vicissim risero.

There is no synaphea between the lines—being *asynartete ;* and, though the hexameter preferably ends with a long syllable, the last syllable of the iambic line is more often short.

In the first of the two Epodes (xiv.) the penthemimeral caesura is observed in the iambic lines, though sometimes with elisions. In the next it is neglected, and lines are found like

> In verba iurabas mea.

The scale of feet is as follows :—

```
∪ ∪ | − ∪ ∪ | − ∪ ∪ | − ∪ ∪ | − ∪ ∪ | − ⏑
− | − − | − − | − − |
∪ − | ∪ − | ∪ − | ∪ ∪ |
− − | − − |
− ∪ ∪ |
```

§ 7. Systema Iambicum

The first ten Epodes are written in pairs of iambic lines, the first of each pair being an ordinary senarius, or trimeter, and the second a dimeter. A series of such pairs is called a *systema iambicum*. The name of *Epode* was itself derived from this tacking on of a shorter line to a longer. Horace, as was before mentioned, called these compositions *iambi*, and their general character is in accordance with the spirit in which their inventor, Archilochus, is said to have used them— "Archilochum proprio rabies armavit iambo."

The rules to which the Latin trimeter is subject differ but little from those of the Greek tragic senarius. The chief variation is in an anapæst being three times admitted into the third place. In keeping with the sharp, invective character of the *iambi*, resolved feet are not numerous, and are due, in several instances, to the requirements of proper names. A dactyl is only six times found in the first place, and twice in the third; an anapæst three times in each; while a tribrach occurs eight times in the second place, and half as many in the third.[1] The cæsura is far more often penthemimeral than hephthemimeral.

In the dimeter, the first and third feet are preferably spondees. Resolved feet, as before, are rare. A tribrach comes once (ii. 62).

Videre properantes domum.

A dactyl is found twice at the beginning, owing to the proper name *Canidia*, which might easily be pronounced as a trisyllable. In v. 100 is a case of hiatus—

Et Esquilinae alites.

If the above remarks are borne in mind, a scale of feet will not be necessary.

[1] Schiller, as before, p. 37.

§ 8. IAMBIC SENARIUS

In one Epode alone (xvii.) Horace employs the iambic trimeter, or senarius, unmixed. His study of Greek models made him subject his lines in this metre to the strict laws of the Greek tragic senarius. Out of the 81 verses of which the piece consist, the spondee is found in 13 instances as the first foot, 56 as the third, and 38 as the fifth. The tribrach is three times in the second place, once in the third, and twice in the fourth. The dactyl is three times in first place, and once in the third.[1] Most of these resolutions are due to proper names. The last syllable is somewhat more often short than long. The cæsura is, with only three exceptions, penthemimeral.

In their fine polish, Horace's iambics stand in strong contrast, for example, to the rude and heavily-weighted lines of Phaedrus. To be used appropriately, they should be chosen as the vehicle for satire and invective. The more eager and acrimonious the attack, the greater will be the proportion of iambic feet to spondees.

§ 9. ON SYNAPHEA IN HORACE

Synaphea, or the linking together of a series of lines in such a way that the feet may be scanned throughout as rigidly as if they formed but one long line, is a principle well known to the reader of a Greek anapaestic chorus. There is also an example of it in Horace, *Od.* iii. 12. As that is a solitary example, we may suppose that Horace did not think it worth the trouble of repeating.

---

[1] Schiller, p. 35.

But while the principle of strict synaphea cannot be applied to the Odes in general, a modified form of it is so generally observed, that there is a growing tendency to look with suspicion on the comparatively few instances where it seems neglected. In all cases, except in that of the Pherecratian line, and in the case of the Ode just mentioned, the last syllable of each verse is allowed to be common (though much oftener long than short); so that there can be no question about the application of *strict* synaphea. But a modification of it, to the extent of not readily allowing a short vowel, or -*um*, to stand at the end of a line, if the next begin with a vowel, is observed by Horace in the Odes to a degree much beyond what many suppose. The subject was partially discussed by Tate, in his *Horatius Restitutus*, and has of late been far more searchingly examined by Dr. Verrall, in his *Studies in Horace*. I will set down all the instances of apparent hiatus, between the end of one line and the beginning of the next, that I have myself noticed in the four Books. The list does not include cases of what has been called *collision*, or the standing unelided of long vowels, or diphthongs, or of the syllables -*am*, -*em*.[1]

A. neve te nostris vitiis iniquum   ocior aura   (i. 2. 47)
B. non tangenda rates transiliunt vada.   Audax omnia (i. 3. 24)
C. leti corripuit gradum. | Expertus vacuum   (i. 3. 33)

---

[1] Horace's practice with regard to elision of long vowels, etc., within the compass of a verse, varied at different times. In the Third Book of the Odes he uses great liberty, eliding *ā* twenty times, *ī* three times, *ē* once, *ae* once. Twelve words in -*m* are also elided in the same Book before a short vowel. In the Fourth Book he becomes stricter again. See Waltz, p. 174.

D. in Iunonis honore | aptum dicit (i. 7. 8)
E. melior fortuna parente | ibimus, o socii (i. 7. 25)
F. cur apricum | oderit campum (i. 8. 3)
G. dum loquimur fugerit invida | aetas (i. 11. 7)
H. Fabriciumque. | Hunc et incomptis (i. 12. 40)
I. fias recantatis amica | opprobriis (i. 16. 27)
J. dis pietas mea | et musa cordist (i. 17. 13)
K. leonum | arida nutrix (i. 22. 15)
L. revisens aequor Atlanticum | impune (i. 31. 14)
M. crine decorum. | Odecus Phoebi (i. 32. 12)
N. militiaeque. | Vnde si Parcae (ii. 6. 8)
O. publica cura. | Expedit matris (ii. 8. 8)
P. litus iniquum. | Auream quisquis (ii. 10. 4)
Q. nocturno cruore | Hospitis (ii. 13. 7)
R. illa venena Colcha | et quidquid usquam (ii. 13. 8)
S. te cadum , in domini caput immerentis (ii. 13. 11)
T. ab omni parte beatum. | Abstulit (ii. 15. 28)
U. columenque rerum. | A, te meae si (ii. 17. 4)
V. tibi praeda cedat maior an illa. , Interim (iii. 20. 8)
W. avis imminentum, | oscinem corvum (iii. 27. 10)
X. victa furore. | Vnde quo veni (iii. 27. 36)
Y. vertice fumum. | Vt tamen noris (iv. 11. 12 .

Of the 25 instances collected above, 12, or nearly half, are defensible on the ground of a distinct pause in the sense. Of the remaining 13, three (D, R, and V) are the subjects of disputed reading (*honorem*, *Colchica*, *illi*). One (H) is obelised by some editors, as by L. Müller. So that not more than 9 cases are left which do not admit of a ready explanation. Solutions have been proposed of the few that remain. But while the probability of some of these may be doubted, the fact remains, that out of the large number of lyrical verses written by Horace, not as many as ten have a short vowel or -*um* left unelided, without an evident reason. How little this abstention has been followed by modern imitators of Horace, a glance at any printed collection of lyrics will show.[1] A few great masters of the art, by a sure instinct have avoided the hiatus.

§ 10. Usage of Words in Horace

Under this heading a few hints may be given, likely to be of use to the learner.[2]

The genitive of nouns in *-ius* or *-ium* is always *-i*, not *-ii*. Thus *Iuli, imperi*, not *Iulii, imperii*. This does not apply to adjectives.

The contracted form of the genitive plural, *-um* for *-orum*, should be limited to the words in which Horace actually uses it, namely *deum, divum, nummum*. In i. 12. 2, *virum* is accusative.

Ast, a convenient form to use before vowels, is not found in the Odes.

No dative singular of the fourth declension is found in Horace.

Di and *dis*, not *dei* and *deis*, are the forms to be used.

Participles in *-ans* or *-ens* make *-ĕ* in the ablative, not *-i*.

The form *diei*, as the genitive of *dies*, is not in the Odes, though Horace has it in the Satires. Vergil has both *die* and *diei*.

Of other nouns of the fifth declension, Horace uses *fidē* for the genitive of *fides*, and *rēi* of *res*.

The perfect tense form in *-ivi* is not in Horace.

---

[1] I am quite aware that in the renderings of the Exercises which follow several violations of this rule will be perceived. As some may still not admit that a rule can be deduced from the facts mentioned above, I have not presumed to alter the work of other scholars.

[2] Most of them are taken from the *Index Grammaticus et Metricus* appended to L. Müller's *Horatius*, 1887.

Haud is not found in the Odes: once in the Epodes, often in the Satires and Epistles.

The pronoun *is, ea, id* is absent from the Odes, except in the genitive form *eius* in two disputed passages (iii. 11. 18 and iv. 8. 18).

Nec, before vowels, is to be preferred to *neque*, unless where the sound would offend the ear, as in i. 6. 5. "Nos Agrippa, neque haec dicere," etc.

Ni occurs once in the Epodes, often in the Satires, etc., but never in the Odes, unless iv. 6. 21 be genuine.

Quis (= *queis*) for *quibus* has no support in the Odes except i. 26. 3 "quis sub Arcto | rex gelidae metuatur orae," where Müller takes it as nominative.

Est should coalesce with a previous vowel by prodelision, as *arduist*.

§ 11. Miscellaneous Idioms

Some usages are common to all Latin poets alike. Such are the use of an adjective, where we should use an adverb, as *laetus excepit*, "he received him gladly"; or the preference of a special to a general term, for picturesqueness, as *notus, auster, zephyrus,* etc., for "wind," *mare Creticum* (or any other) for "sea," and the like.

What is most noticeable in Horace is the class of idioms generally known as Grecisms. As he finished his studies in Athens, and is constantly praising the *exemplaria Graeca*, it was natural that his style should get tinctured by them. The following are some of the most prominent, in the Odes:[1]—

[1] For a full and elaborate account of them, the reader is referred to

(*a*) The genitive after verbs, where the ablative would be otherwise used, as in iii. 27. 69, *abstineto . . . irarum* (while in the *Ars Poet.* it is *abstinuit venere et vino*); ii. 9. 17, *Desine mollium . . . querellarum;* ii. 13. 38, *decipitur laborum,* etc.

(*b*) The genitive after adjectives and participles, where we should in like manner expect an ablative; as in iii. 17. 16, *cum famulis operum solutis;* i. 22, 1, "*scelerisque purus.*"

(*c*) The infinitive after adjectives and participles, instead of a gerund, or some prepositional construction; as ii. 4. 11, *leviora tolli Pergama;* iv. 2. 59, *niveus videri;* ii. 18. 38, *levare . . . vocatus;* iii. 29. 50, *ludum insolentem ludere pertinax;* Carm. Saec. 25, *veraces cecinisse.*

(*d*) A like infinitive after verbs, instead of the gerundive, as in i. 12. 2, *quem virum . . . sumis celebrare;* i. 26. 3, *tradam protervis . . . portare ventis.* (On this complementary or "prolative" infinitive, see Waltz, p. 127.)

Male is a favourite word with Horace, who uses it with adjectives and participles in various senses: *digito male pertinaci* (i. 9. 24), "feigning resistance" (Bentley); *male dispari* (i. 17. 25), intensifying the force of the adjective; *male ominatis* (iii. 14. 11), giving a bad or negative meaning; *male feriatos* (iv. 6. 14), "keeping ill-timed holiday" (Wickham).

the chapter on "Hellénisme d'Horace," in Waltz's *Des Variations,* etc., before quoted.

⁎ Words in brackets are not to be translated. Words in italics are to come in the following line.

EXERCISE I[1]

Under the greenwood tree
Who loves to lie with me,
And tune his merry note
Unto the sweet bird's throat,
Come hither, come hither, come hither;
Here shall he see no enemy
But winter and rough weather.

Who doth ambition shun,
And loves to lie in the sun,
Seeking the food he eats,
And pleased with what he gets,
Come hither, come hither, come hither;
Here shall he see no enemy
But winter and rough weather.

        Shakspeare.

Retranslation

I

Who loves, haunting the woods along with me, (2) to lie stretched in idleness beneath the leafy shade, (3, 4) awaking strains in unison with the sweet throat of birds?

[1] Exercises I.-XX. are in Sapphic metre. See the Introduction, p. xxiv.

Hither let him come, let him but come ; (2) let no delay keep back too much those who hear my thrice-repeated call ; (3, 4) here winter alone is to be dreaded, or the air rough with storms.

III

Whoever *shuns* courting the breath of popular applause, (2) a lover of basking ease ; (3) so long as he provides his own sustenance, with sparing (4) lot content,

IV

hither let him come, let him but come ; (2) let no delay keep back those who hear my thrice-repeated call ; (3, 4) here winter alone is to be dreaded, or the air rough with storms.

Hints

I. (1) "Who loves," *quem juvat;* "to haunt," *colēre;* "woods": use the resolved form of *silva*, as in Hor. *Od.* i. 23. 4 ; (2) "to lie stretched :" comp. Hor. *Od.* i. 1. 22 ; "in idleness," *vacuus;* (3) "in unison with," *consonus* (with abl.)

II. (1) "Let him come," *adsit;* (2) "no delay," *nil morae;* "those who hear" (acc. partic.) ; "my thrice-repeated call," lit. "(me) thrice calling," to come at the end of line 2 ; (3) "is to be dreaded," (*est*) *gravis;* (4) "rough :" comp. Hor. *Od.* ii. 9. 1, "*hispidos* manant in agros."

III. (1) "Courting," *ambitus* (with genit.) ; "the breath of popular applause :" comp. Hor. *Od.* iii. 2. 20, "arbitrio popularis aurae ;" (2) "a lover of," *studiosus* (with genit.) ; (3) "so long as," *dum* (with subj.) ; "his own," *suos . . . ipse;* (4) "content with ": comp. Hor. *Od.* ii. 18. 14, "satis *beatus* unicis Sabinis."

IV. (See notes on II.)

EXERCISE II

Sweet is the song of rivulets descending,
Sweet the light whisper of the breezy woodland,
Murmur of bees and melody of songsters
     Hid in the bushes.

Grant me, O fate, some covert in the forest,
Far from the strife and trouble of the city,
Where my tired eyes and sorrow-laden spirit
     Peace may revisit.
         C. S.

RETRANSLATION

I

Sweet (is) the sound of falling waters, (2) sweetly do the Zephyrs whisper through the wood; (3) or else the hum of bees, and the song of bird (4) hidden in the leaves.

II

Be there given to me a covert with secluded shade, (2) far away from the restless turmoil of the city, (3) where peace my weary eyes (acc.) and sad (4) heart may revisit.

HINTS

I. (1) "Waters," *undae*; (2) "sweetly" (neut. of adj.); (4) "leaves," *frons*.

II. (1) "Covert," *tegmen*; (2) "far away," *amotum*.

Here sleeps my babe in silence,
    Heaven's his rest:
For God takes soonest those
    He loveth best.

Epitaph in Rainham Churchyard.

RETRANSLATION

Here a dear infant beneath the silent ground (2) sleeps: the powers above (are) the givers of (his) rest: (3, 4) for God takes away more quickly from us those dearer to Himself.

HINTS

(1) "Ground," *humus*; (2) "powers above," *superi*; "givers," lit. "authors," *auctores*; (3) "those dearer," *cariores*; "more quickly," *ocius*.

EXERCISE III

Like an army defeated
The snow hath retreated,
And now it doth fare ill
On the top of the bare hill.
The ploughboy is whooping anon! anon!
    There's joy in the mountains,
    There's life in the fountains;
    Small clouds are sailing,
    Blue sky prevailing;
The rain is over and gone.

WORDSWORTH.

RETRANSLATION

I

Like as battalions fly scattered, (2) the snow is driven away and has retreated, and on the barren hill (3) has fared badly: now, in youth (4) exulting, the ploughman

II

cries Anon! to the meadow, and as oft the plain (2) re-echoes Anon! on all sides; a new vigour crowns (3) the mountains with gladness, a new life the fountain's (4) stream (acc.) calls forth.

III

As barks are wafted swiftly on by the sail, (2) lo! the clouds lightly fly, and *an azure* colour (3) prevails in the sky, and *shines clear*, the showers (4) being driven away.

HINTS

I. (1) "Battalion," *phălanx, -ngis*; "scattered," *fusus*; (2) "is driven away and," *pulsa* (with main verb); (3) "has fared badly," lit. "has managed its own affairs badly."

II. (1) "Anon," *heus*; (2) "re-echoes," *reddit*; "on all sides," *passim*; (4) "call forth," *excito*.

III. (1) "Waft on," *fero*; "swiftly" (adj.); (4) "shine clear," *splendeo*.

EXERCISE IV

What ailed thee, Robin, that thou couldst pursue
    A beautiful creature
    That is gentle by nature?

Beneath the summer sky
From flower to flower let him fly;
'Tis all he wishes to do.
The cheerer thou of our indoor sadness,
He is the friend of our summer gladness;
What hinders, then, that ye should be
    Playmates in the sunny weather,
    And fly about in the air together?
His beautiful bosom is drest
    In crimson as bright as thine own.
If thou wouldst be happy in thy nest,
O pious bird, whom man loves best,
    Love him, or leave him alone.

WORDSWORTH.

RETRANSLATION

I

What aileth thee, O bird of ruddy breast? (2) Why didst thou take a malicious pleasure in pursuing a prey (3) that flies fair in form, and in disposition (4) harmful to none?

II

The summer sky is smiling; let it wander (2) everywhere among the roses; that is enough to the roamer. (3) Thou canst cheer (one) in sadness, whoever (4) is shut up indoors.

III

It is present (as) a companion to the joyful (one), as through the *summer* field (2) he wanders on foot: what shall forbid (3) that in united sport through the sunny (4) lands ye fly?

IV

Lo! the air of heaven lies open to you both alike; (2) nor is *its* ruddy *breast* inferior to thy colour, (3) and with like *markings* glows (4) (its) purple.

V

So may thy nest be prosperous for thee, pious (bird), (2) specially loved by human affections: (3) love it, or else at least let it roam without thee (4) in freedom o'er the plains.

HINTS

I. (1) "What aileth thee," *quid tibi est?* "of ruddy," etc., *rubicunda*, with acc. of nearer definition; (2) "take a malicious pleasure in," *male gestio*, with inf.; (3) "disposition," *indoles* (acc.)

II. (1) "Sky," *polus*; "it" (emphat.); (3) "cheer," *recreo*; (4) "indoors," *intus*.

III. (1) "It" (emphat.); (2) "on foot," *pede*; (3) "that," *quominus*; "lands," *rura*.

IV. (1) "Both alike," *simul*; "ruddy," *rutilus*; "is inferior to," *cedit* (with dat.); "like," *par*; (4) "markings," *signa*.

V. (1) "Prosperous," *beatus*; (2) "specially," *unice*; "affections," *studia*; (4) "in freedom" (adj.)

EXERCISE V

The heart of childhood is all mirth;
  We frolic to and fro,
As free and blithe as if on earth
  Were no such thing as woe.

KEBLE.

Retranslation

The age of childhood plays idly, (2) wanders to and fro, and rejoices with a mind (3) free, as though of tears and evils (4) life were devoid.

Hints

(1) "Of childhood" (adj.); "idly," *incassum*; (2) "to and fro," *huc illuc*; (3) "as though," *tamquam* (with subj.); (4) "to be devoid of," *carere* (with abl.).

Dreams

Here we are all, by day; by night we're hurled
By dreams each one into a several world.
HERRICK.

Retranslation

Here we are, while daylight favours; but on a sudden (2) black night comes to us, and in a dream (3) we are each hurried through diverse shores (4) and realms of the universe.

Hints

(1) "Daylight," *lux*; (4) "universe," *mundus*.

To Enjoy the Time

While fates permit us, let's be merry;
Pass all we must the fatal ferry;
And this our life too whirls away
With the rotation of the day.
HERRICK.

RETRANSLATION

While it is allowed us, let us jest merrily; (2) the ferry of death must be crossed by all; (3) life is whirling on, as *the orbit* of the day (4) revolves.

HINTS

(1) "Merrily" (adj.), *hilares*; (2) "ferry," "ford," *vada* (n. pl.); (3) "is whirling on," *torquetur*; "of the day" (adj.)

EXERCISE VI

Sweet Echo, sweetest nymph, that liv'st unseen
    Within thy airy shell,
By slow Mæander's margent green,
    And in the violet-embroider'd vale,
    Where the love-lorn nightingale
    Nightly to thee her sad song mourneth well,
Canst thou not tell me of a gentle pair

That likest thy Narcissus are?
    Or, if thou have
    Hid them in some flowery cave,
Tell me but where,
Sweet queen of parley, daughter of the sphere!
So may'st thou be translated to the skies,
And give resounding grace to all heaven's harmonies.
                                MILTON.

RETRANSLATION

I

(1, 2) Nymph, whom the bank of Mæander rippling

with gentle stream holds, and of moist (3, 4) cloud a shell confines, lurking on green margent:

II

or in shady and violet-embroidered (2) vale, where along with thee Philomela (her) complaints (3) duly redoubles by night, with faithful (4) grief overcome:

III

Is the gentle *pair* of brothers known to thee; (2) such as recall the form of thy (3) Narcissus, goddess? for whom, O *daughter* of the arching (4) heaven,

IV

if beneath any flowery grot in the woods (2) thou hast spread a couch, tell me in kindness; (3) whether thou art pleased to be called a goddess, or of the musical (4) tongue a mistress.

V

So mayest thou both return to thy native sky, (2) and, so long as thou *minglest* in the strains of the nine-fold choir (3, 4) a winged (visitant), may their joys be redoubled for the gods themselves.

HINTS

I. (1) "Rippling," *trepidantis*; (2) "of" (sign of abl.): comp. also Hor. *Od.* iv. 2. 30; (3) "shell," *testudo*; (4) "confines," *cingit* (last word of stanza).

II. (1) "Violet-embroidered," *violis picta* (comp. also Hor. *Od.* i. 12. 5); (3 "by night," *nocturnus*.

III. (1) "Gentle," *genialis*; (3) "arching," *rotundus*.

IV. (1) "In the woods," lit. "of the woods," *nemorum*; (2) "hast spread" (pf. subj.); "in kindness," *benigna*; (3) "art pleased," etc.: comp. Hor. *Sat.* ii. 6. 20, "seu Iane libentius audis;" "musical," *canorus*; (4) "mistress," *arbitra*.

V. (1) Comp. Hor. *Od.* i. 2. 46, "Serus in caelum redeas," etc.: (2) "so long as" = "provided that," *dum* with subj.; "nine-fold," *novenus*; (3) "winged," *ales*: comp. Hor. *Od.* i. 2. 42; "mingle," *interesse*.

EXERCISE VII

Upon Love

I held Love's head while it did ache;
    But so it chanced to be,
The cruel pain did him forsake,
    And forthwith came to me.

Ah me! how shall my grief be still'd?
    Or where else shall we find
One like to me, who must be kill'd
    For being too too kind?

                      HERRICK.

RETRANSLATION

I

It chanced that Love was once in pain; and his head (acc.) (2) I sat by and held while he was ill: (3) soon the cruel pain left the god, and straightway (4) I myself was smarting.

II

Who will be able to ease my grief? (2) or where is another to be provided for me (3, 4) to whom in truth, smarting, ah! too much, death is a merciful lot?

Hints

I. (1) "It chanced that," *fors*; (2) "I sat by and," *adsidens* (with main verb); "held" (descriptive present); "while he was ill," lit. "of him ill," *aegri*; (3) "straightway," *ilicet*.

II. (1) "My" (dat. of ind. obj.); (2) "to be provided," *comparandus*; (3, 4) "in truth," "in fact," *quippe* (line 4); "merciful," *benignus*.

EXERCISE VIII

Prière

Ah! si vous saviez comme on pleure
De vivre seul et sans foyers,
Quelquefois devant ma demeure
      Vous passeriez.

Si vous saviez ce que fait naître
Dans l'âme triste un pur regard,
Vous regarderiez ma fenêtre
      Comme au hasard.

Si vous saviez quel baume apporte
Au cœur la présence d'un cœur,
Vous vous assoiriez sous ma porte
      Comme une sœur.

Si vous saviez que je vous aime,
Surtout si vous saviez comment,
Vous entreriez peut-être même
   Tout simplement.
         SULLY PRUDHOMME.

RETRANSLATION

I

Pyrrha, if thou knewest with what *complaints* I am ever *deploring* a life (2) of celibacy, devoid of a settled home, (3, 4) thou would'st turn thy steps near my dwelling.

II

Didst thou really know what and whence in the *sad* heart (2) of (him) who once gazes on thee, *thy look* arouses, (3) thou mightest this my window (acc.) just as (4) by chance look at.

III

How efficacious a remedy (acc.) to a sick *heart* brings (2) a heart, were it not unknown to thee, (3) at my doors *like* a gentle sister (4) thou would'st sit.

IV

If thou knewest that I am inflamed with a passion for thee, (2) Pyrrha; if, how much thy fire consumes me, (3) thou moreover knewest; laying aside bashfulness, (4) thou would'st perchance enter.

HINTS

I. (1) "Knewest," *nosses;* "complaint," *questus* (in line 3); "ever," *usque,* "deplore," *ploro* (in line 3); (2) "of celibacy," *caelebs;* "home," *lar;* "devoid of," *destitutus;* (3) "turn," *fero;* (4) "dwelling," *limen* (pl.).

II. (1) "Really," *satis;* (2) "of him who gazes," *intuentis;* (3) "look," *vultus;* (3, 4) "this my," *hanc . . . mihi;* "just as . . . by chance," *sic . . . forte:* comp. Hor. *Od.* ii. 11. 14, "iacentes sic temere;" "look at," *tueor.*

III. (1) "Efficacious," *praesens;* (2) begin with *pectori pectus;* "were it not unknown to," *nisi . . . lateret;* (4) "like," *more* (with gen.)

IV. (1) "Am inflamed," *calco;* "a passion for thee," *tua . . . fax;* (2) "consume," *uro;* (3) "moreover," *insuper;* "bashfulness," *pudor.*

EXERCISE IX

She dwelt among the untrodden ways,
    Beside the springs of Dove,
A maid whom there were none to praise,
    And very few to love.

A violet by a mossy stone,
    Half hidden from the eye;
Fair as a star, when only one
    Is shining in the sky.

She lived unknown, and few could know
    When Lucy ceased to be;
But she is in her grave, and oh!
    The difference to me.

WORDSWORTH.

Retranslation

I

Lalage lived by the bubbling springs (2) of Dēvāna, dwelling in untrodden ways; (3) whom with rare footstep a suitor, with rarer (4) a flatterer, used to approach.

II

But she grew up in seclusion, like a violet (2) lying hid behind a mossy stone; (3) bright as in the depths of the pure heaven (4) a star shining.

III

She flourished, a maiden of obscure lot; (2) she passed away, her lot scarce known; but alas! (3) in place of buried hope there now remain to me how many (4) wearinesses of life!

Hints

I. (2) "Untrodden ways," *non trita . . . viarum*.

II. (1) "In seclusion," *reducta;* "like:" comp. Hor. *Od.* iii. 14. 1, *Herculis ritu;* (3) "bright as," *sic nitens . . . velut;* "in the depths of," *ima*, agreeing with *stella*.

III. (1) "Of obscure lot:" for the genit. comp. Hor. *Od.* i. 9. 7, "*multi Lydia nominis;*" "pass away," *pereo*.

EXERCISE X

Ask me no more: the moon may draw the sea;
   The cloud may stoop from heaven and take the shape,
  With fold to fold, of mountain or of cape:
But, O too fond, when have I answered thee?
                Ask me no more.

Ask me no more: what answer should I give?
I love not hollow cheek or faded eye:
Yet, O my friend, I will not have thee die!
Ask me no more, lest I should bid thee live;
                Ask me no more.

Ask me no more: thy fate and mine are seal'd:
I strove against the stream, and all in vain;
Let the great river take me to the main;
No more, dear love, for at a touch I yield;
                Ask me no more.
                    TENNYSON.

RETRANSLATION

I

Cease at length from entreaty: the moon may draw the sea, (2) and a flitting cloud, gliding from the sky, (3) *may take up* in its folds a mountain's heights or the sea (4) shores.

II

When, however, *am I proved* to have surrendered myself to thee? (2) Why, what, infatuated one, didst thou wish? (3) Avoid beseeching one struggling much, (4) denying much.

III

A wasting cheek displeases (me), and so does (2) a faded countenance: but, O loving one, what am I to dare? (3) *To thee*, who would'st die for me against my will, am I even (4) to give life?

IV

Naught heed I: beloved one! 'tis over with us both. (2) Let the great river draw (me), vainly striving, (3) into the sea. O spare to ask often; *by one* touch (4) I am vanquished.

HINTS

I. (1) "Cease from," *absisto* (pres. subj.); "may" (*est ut* is understood with the verb in this line, and *estque ut* begins line 2); (2) "flitting," *vagus*; (3) "take up," with the idea of "enfolding," "stealing over," *occupo*, as in "sopor occupat artus;" "folds," "windings," *flexus*; "sea" (adj.) *marinus*.

II. (2) "Am proved," *arguor*; "why, what," *quid enim*; (3) "avoid," *fuge*; "beseeching," *supplicare* (with dat.); "much" (neut. pl. adj.)

III. (1) "Wasting," *tabens*; "and so does" (repeat *displicent*, with *que*); (2) "faded," *marcidus* (pl.); "am I to dare," *ausim*; (3) "against my will," *invitus* (dat.); "even," *ultro*: comp. Ter. *Phor.* ii. 2. 13, "O audaciam, etiam me ultro accusatum venit!"

IV. (1) "Naught heed I," *nil moror*; "'tis over with," *actum est* (with dat. of ind. object); "us both," *duobus*: (2) "vainly" (see note on "much," II. 3); (3) "ask often," *rogito*: comp. Verg. *Aen.* i. 750, "multa super Priamo rogitans;" "by one," *ab uno*. For this use of the preposition, when not applied to a personal agent, comp. Sall. *Iug.* c. 31, "ut vobis animus ab ignavia atque socordia corruptus sit."

EXERCISE XI

"A weary lot is thine, fair maid,
    A weary lot is thine!
To pull the thorn thy brow to braid,
    And press the rue for wine.
A lightsome eye, a soldier's mien,
    A feather of the blue,

C

　　　　　A doublet of the Lincoln green—
　　　　　　　No more of me you knew,
　　　　　　　　　　My love!
　　　　　　　No more of me you knew!

"This morn is merry June, I trow,
　　　The rose is budding fain;
　But she shall bloom in winter snow
　　　Ere we two meet again."
　He turn'd his charger as he spake
　　　Upon the river shore;
　He gave his bridle-reins a shake,
　　　Said, "Adieu for evermore,
　　　　　　　　　My love!
　　　And adieu for evermore!"
　　　　　　　　　　　　Scott.

Retranslation

I

"O thou that must grieve for a too hard lot! (2) whom, lurking (nom.) beneath the garland twined-round (thee), (3) a thorn, whom (when) pressing-out wine, false (4) rue beguiled,

II

"Thee the light laugh and the green doublet (2) of the soldier, and the ornament of his glancing plume (3) deluded, ah! unskilled (voc. fem.) as yet to suspect (4) a baser one.

III

"Now, Phoebus bringing back festive days, (2) the flower of the rose is swelling: but it will bloom (3) amid the snows, ere that us separated (acc.) a kindly (4) hour shall have joined.

IV

"Live thrice happy, Lalagē!" (2) he said: "farewell for ever;" and at the same time (3) gives the rein to his steeds wheeled-about, leaving (4) the margin of the bank.

HINTS

I. (1) "Thou that must grieve for," fut. partic. of *doleo*; (2) "lurking:" comp. Hor. *Od.* iii. 12. 11, "latitantem fruticeto... aprum;" "twined round thee," *innexus*; (3) "wine," *merum* · "false," *mentita*.

II. (2) "Doublet," *thorax*; for the epithet, comp. Juv. *Sat.* xi. 198, "eventum viridis quo colligo panni;" (2) "glancing," *coruscus*; (3) "unskilled as yet," *nondum cata* with infin.: comp. Hor. *Od.* iii. 12. 10, "catus... cervos jaculari;" (4) "a baser one," *deteriorem*.

III. (1) "Bringing back:" comp. Hor. *Od.* iii. 29. 20, "sole dies referente siccos," and iv. 6. 42; (3) "amid," *per*; "ere that,' *prius* (in line 2) *quam*.

IV. (1) "Thrice," *ter* ... *quaterque*, for which *bis terque, ter et quater* are also found in Horace; (2) "for ever," *aeternum*: comp. Verg. *Aen.* vi. 617, "sedet aeternumque sedebit;" (3) "wheeled about," *conversus*; "leaving" (abl. absol. pass.).

EXERCISE XII

Tell me, thou star, whose wings of light
Speed thee in thy fiery flight,
In what caverns of the night
      Will thy pinions close now?

Tell me, moon, thou pale and gray
Pilgrim of heaven's homeless way,
In what depth of night and day
      Seekest thou repose now?

Weary wind, who wanderest,
Like the world's rejected guest,
Hast thou still some secret nest
      Of the tree or billow?

SHELLEY.

RETRANSLATION

I

Star! whom (thy) flashing pinions hurry on, (2) speeding in fiery course, say to (me) asking (3) in what cave of night closed at length does thy (4) wing repose?

II

Moon! that traversest the vacant heaven, (2) a pilgrim pale with weary aspect, (3) prithee say what retreat gives rest (4) by night or by day.

III

Wind! that fliest everywhere in weariness, (2) to whom none careth to unbar (his) doors, (3, 4) does any tree or billow foster thee in secret nest?

HINTS

I. (1) "Pinion," *pinna*; "hurry on," *rapio*; (2) "speeding," *citus*; (3) "cave," *specus*; "thy," *tibi*; (4 "repose," *quiesco*.

II. (1) "Traverse," *pererro* (2) "pilgrim," *peregrina*; "pale," *pallens*; (3) "prithee," *precor*; "retreat," *recessus*; (4) "or by day," *dieve*.

III. (1) "Fliest," *volitas*; "in weariness" (adj.); (2) "unbar," *resero*; (3) "does," (begin with *Tene*); "foster," *foveo*.

EXERCISE XIII

The praise of Bacchus then the sweet musician sung,
Of Bacchus ever fair and ever young;
    The jolly god in triumph comes,
    Sound the trumpets, beat the drums!
    Flushed with a purple grace
    He shows his honest face;
Now give the hautboys breath; he comes, he comes!

    Bacchus, ever fair and young,
        Drinking joys did first ordain;
    Bacchus' blessings are a treasure,
    Drinking is the soldier's pleasure:
        Rich the treasure,
        Sweet the pleasure;
    Sweet is pleasure after pain.

                      DRYDEN.

RETRANSLATION

I

Then in sweet praise and measures the poet (2) sings the glory of Bacchus: ever fair (3), lo! ever lusty is Bacchus in the primal (4) flower of youth.

II

Now the god comes hither in joyous triumph : (2) let the trumpets give voice, let a new *force* of drums (3) thunder on all sides: ruddiness and beauty (4) mark the beauteous

III

face of the god : now, now fill ye the reeds (2) with breath; Bacchus comes, ever fair (3), ever rejoicing comes he in the primal (4) flower of youth.

IV

Who rather than Bacchus, is said to have laid down (2) the agreements and merry laws of drinking? (3) So does treasure grow well; the soldier (acc.) (4) an ample pleasure

V

from this source makes happy : assuredly it is a rich treasure ; (2) oh! assuredly a sweet pleasure is afforded from this; (3, 4) a sweet pleasure rightly follows pain (when) driven away.

Hints

I. (1) " Measures," *numeri* ; (2) " ever," *usque* ; (3) " is lusty," *viget* ; (3) " primal," *primaevus*.

II. (3) " Force," *vis*. Note this use of *vis* with gen. to express " a quantity of," "a number of:" comp. Hor. *Od*. iv. 11. 4, " est hederae vis multa ;" (3) " on all sides," *passim* ; " beauty, *venustas* ; (4) " mark" (sing.) ; " beauteous," *honestus*: comp. Verg. *Georg*. iv. 232, " Taygete simul os terris ostendit honestum Pleias."

III. (1) " Face," *ora* ; " reed," *calamus*.

IV. (1) " Rather than," sooner than," *prior* ; " is said," *fertur* ; (2) " agreement," *foedus* ; (3) " So does," etc. : comp. for the sense 1 *Esdras*, iii. 21 ; " the soldier," lit. " one on service," *militantem*.

V. (1) " From this source," *hinc* ; " makes happy," *beat* ; " rich," *opulentus* ; (3) " when driven away," *exactum*.

EXERCISE XIV

Fairy Queen!
Fairy Queen!
Mortal steps are on the green;
Come away!
Haste away!
Fairies, guard your Queen!
Hither, hither, fairy Queen!
Lest thy silvery wing be seen;
O'er the sky
Fly, fly, fly!
Fairies, guard your lady Queen!
O'er the sky
Fly, fly, fly!
Fairies, guard your Queen!

Fairy Queen!
Fairy Queen!
Mortal steps no more are seen;
Now we may
Down and play
O'er the daisied green.
Lightly, lightly, fairy Queen!
Trip it gently on the green!
Fairies gay,
Trip away
Round about your lady Queen!
Fairies gay,
Trip away
Round about your Queen.

GAMMER GRETHEL.

RETRANSLATION

I

Goddess, that singly rulest all the nymphs, (2) lo! profane mortals with (their) feet (3) are trampling the turf: 'tis time to hasten, (4) time to depart.

II

Goddess, we must quickly withdraw: do ye take care, (2) Naiads, lest perchance there be seen the wing (3) rivalling silver: with rapid flight (4) o'ertop the sky.

III

Goddess, that rulest the nymphs, lo! nowhere (2) is any longer seen men's footstep o'er the greensward; (3) leave thou the sky; thou and thine may (4) sport on the *daisied* mead.

IV

In joy lightly *lead ye* the dances (2) on the plains, and with merry movement (3) let the light foot trip, and do ye attendants your (4) goddess surround.

Hints

I. (1) Comp. Hor. *Od.* i. 35. 1, "O diva, gratum quae regis Antium;" "all" (=all together), *cunctus*.

II. (1) "Withdraw," *cedo;* (3) "rivalling," *aemulus* (with gen.); (4) "o'ertop," "gain the heights of," *vinco*.

III. (2) "Footstep," *planta;* "o'er the greensward," *per herbas;* (3) "may," *fas (est)*, with dat.; (4) "daisied," *floridus* (to come in IV. 1).

IV. (1) "In joy" (adj.); "dance," *chorea;* (2) "merry," *hilaris;* (3) "trip," *salto;* "your" (to be translated).

EXERCISE XV

Go rouse the deer with horn and hound,
    And chase him o'er the mountains free;
Or bid the hollow woods resound
    The triumph of your archery.

Pan leads: and if you hail me right
    As guardian of the silvan reign,
I'll wing your arrows on their flight,
    And speed your coursers o'er the plain.

              MERIVALE (*from Leonidas*).

RETRANSLATION

I

Go ye, chase over the bare mountains (2) the hind roused with horn and hounds; (3) or *pierce* the hollow woods with the far-resounding (4) bowstring.

II

Go ye: but if ye rightly worship *Pan the guardian* of the groves, (2) under my guidance the arrows (3) shall fly unerringly, and the victorious *hoof* shall scour (4) the plain.

HINTS

I. (1) "Chase," *agito*; "bare," *vastus*; (2) "roused," *excitus*; (3) "far-resounding," *late resonans*; (4) "pierce," *rumpo*.

II. (1) "Worship," *colo* (fut.); (2) "under my guidance," *duce me*; (3) "shall fly" (fut. pft.); "unerringly" (adj.); "scour," *rapio*.

The misty clouds, that fall sometime
    And overcast the skies,
Are like to troubles of our time,
    Which do but dim our eyes.

But as such dews are dried up quite
    When Phoebus shows his face,
So are sad fancies put to flight
    When God doth guide by grace.

                          GASCOIGNE.

RETRANSLATION

I

As mists at times the serene *smiles* (acc.) of the sky (2) overcast, so do life's losses (3) often *overshadow* laughing eyes with rising (4) clouds.

II

And as the vapours are dried up and flee (2) when Phoebus brings back his golden countenance, (3, 4) so does the grace of heaven benignly chase away overshadowing cares.

HINTS

I. (1) "Mist," *nebula*; "sky," *polus*; (2) "overcast," *obruo*; (3) "rising," *obortus*; (4) "overshadow," *umbro*.

II. (1) "Are dried up and" (partic. and verb); (2) "when ... brings" (abl. abs.); (3) "benignly" (adj.); "overshadowing," *obumbrans*.

EXERCISE XVI

Up to our altars, then,
    Haste we, and summon
Courage and loveliness,
    Manhood and woman!
Deep let our pledges be:
    Freedom for ever!
Truce with oppression,
    Never, oh! never.
By our own birthright gift,
    Granted of Heaven,
Freedom for heart and lip
    Be the pledge given!

If we have whisper'd truth,
    Whisper no longer;
Speak as the tempest does,
    Sterner and stronger;
Still be the tones of truth
    Louder and firmer,
Startling the haughty South
    With the deep murmur:
God and our charter's right,
    Freedom for ever!
Truce with oppression,
    Never, oh! never.

                    WHITTIER.

RETRANSLATION

I

Let us hasten, then, to the altars of the Gods. (2) Whoever has martial energy, hither let him *come* at the summons; (3, 4) and whoever is adorned with beauty in the flower of youth.

II

That soon, bound by a weightier vow, (2) we may devote ourselves for evermore to thee, (3) holy Freedom, and there may be peace in no (4) way for tyrants.

III

Let each claim for himself the gift of heaven, (2) and the lot which (his) natal hour brought: that, what rises in his mind, none forbidding, (4) with voice he should relate.

IV

If with lips too closed hitherto the truth (acc.) (2) we have told, no longer let us be ashamed to speak out; (3) but with clear voice, like a rising (4) storm's first

V

murmurs, let *Truth* utter weightier (words), (2) speaking forth (something) more certain, (3) such as *to scare* even a Southern people's haughty (4) cities.

VI

So long as the powers above guard (our) rights for us, (2) be it ever our pleasure to be called free; (3, 4) but let there be no peace henceforward for cruel tyrants.

Hints

I. (1) "Then," *ergo;* (2) "whoever has," *si cui (est)*; "energy," *vigor;* "at the summons" (= "called"); (3) "let him come," *adsit;* "whoever" (fem.); "is adorned with" (take the active turn).

II. (1) "Bound," *adstrictus:* comp. Ov. *Her.* xvi. 320; (2) "ourselves," *nos;* "devote," *dedico;* (3) "and . . . in no," *neque . . . ullo;* (4) "way," *mos.*

III. (1) "Of heaven," *divom;* (2) "bring," *fero;* (3) "that, what," etc. (begin with the rel.); (4) "relate," *refero* (imp. subj.)

IV. (1) "closed lips:" comp. Verg. *Aen.* vi. 155, "pressoque obmutuit ore;" (2) "no longer," *non jam;* "speak out," *profari;* (3) "rising," *ingruens.*

V. (2) "Truth" (personified), *Veritas*, as in Hor. *Od.* i. 24. 7; (2) "speak forth," *eloqui:* comp. Hor. *Od.* iii. 3. 17, "gratum elocuta consiliantibus Iunone divis;" (3) "such as to," *quale* (with subj.)

VI. (1) "Powers above," *superi;* (3) "henceforward," *veniens in aevum.*

EXERCISES XVII, XVIII

Last night, above the whistling wind,
    I heard the welcome rain,—
A fusillade upon the roof,
    A tattoo on the pane :
The keyhole piped, the chimney-top
    A warlike trumpet blew ;
Yet, mingling with these sounds of strife,
    A softer voice stole through.

"Give thanks, O brothers," said the voice,
    "That He who sent the rains
Hath spared your fields the scarlet dew
    That drips from patriot veins :
I've seen the grass on Eastern graves

In brighter verdure rise;
But, oh! the rain that gave it life
 Sprang first from human eyes.

"I come to wash away no stain
 Upon your wasted lea;
I raise no banners, save the ones
 The forest waves to me.
Upon the mountain side, where spring
 Her farthest picket sets,
My réveille awakes a host
 Of grassy bayonets.

"I visit every humble roof,
 I mingle with the low;
Only upon the highest peaks
 My blessings fall in snow:
Until, in tricklings of the stream,
 And drainings of the lea,
My unspent bounty comes at last
 To mingle with the sea."

BRET HARTE.

RETRANSLATION

I

Mastering (acc.) the whistlings of the rising wind, (2) I gladly heard the sound of falling (3) rain, but yesternight, and the *beating* on the summit of (4) the roof;

II

while the drop patters on the rattling windows, (2) and

the concealed crevice of the doors whistles; (3) the hall re-echoing with the winds, like *trumpets* in actual (4) war.

III

Yet still, in the midst of the storm's commotion, a voice (2) of more gentleness seemed to reach my ears: (3, 4) "Return thanks, brothers"—for such you might deem its exhortation—

IV

"for that God, who gives the drops of rain, (2) has not as yet dyed your fields with bloody (3) dew, nor does *the breast* of (one) defending his country trickle (4) with blood.

V

If o'er Eastern plains with richer (2) turf the mounds of the slain grow green, (3) yet a fount gushing from human eyes (4) nourishes the greensward.

VI

Not to fields laid waste by arms am I come, (2) to wash out stains of slaughter; nor any (3) standards, excepting *the leaves* of the forest waving (4) in the blast,

VII

do I lift up for war. O'er the distant slopes, (2) where spring at her farthest outpost far off (3) keeps ward, innumerable spear-points (acc.) (4) at morn o'er the turf

VIII

does my summoning voice arm: but not *despising* the cottages (2) of the poor, or lowly company, (3) only on lofty summits, bountiful with snow (4) my gifts do I pour;

IX

until, what remains of my kindly moisture (2) the tricklings of the spring carry away, or watery (3) valleys drain, quickly destined (4) to the waves of the sea.

Hints

I. (1) "Master," *vinco;* "whistlings:" comp. Verg. *Ecl.* v. 82, "venientis sibilus austri;" (2) "gladly" (adj.); (3) "rain," *imber;* "but," *modo;* "on" (sign of genit.); (4) "beating," *verbera* (pl.)

II. (1) "Patter," *crepito;* "rattling," lit. "struck;" (2) "crevice," *foramen;* (3) "re-echo," *reboo;* "actual," *ipse;* (4) "trumpets," *classica* (pl.)

III. (1) "In the midst of," *mixto;* (2) "of more gentleness," lit. "more gentle;" "to reach," *remeare ad;* (3) "thanks," *gratiae;* "its exhortation," lit. "(it) to have exhorted," *monuisse.*

IV. (1) "Drops," lit. "waters," *liquores;* "of rain" (adj.); (2) "dye," *inficio;* (3) "trickle," *stillo.*

V. (1) "O'er," *per;* "richer," lit. "preferable," *potior;* (2) "of the slain" (dat. of ind. object); (3) "gushing from," *obortus;* (4) "greensward," *gramen* (pl.)

VI. (1) "Laid waste:" comp. Hor. *Od.* iii. 5. 24, "et arva Marte coli *populata* nostro;" (2) "wash out," *eluo;* (3) "excepting," *praeterquam;* "forest," *silva* (in resolved form).

VII. (1) "For war," *martia* (agreeing with *signa* above); "slopes," *iuga;* (2) "outpost," *statio;* (3) "keep ward," *excubo,* "spear-point," "blade" (of corn, etc.), *spica;* (4) "turf," *herba.*

VIII. (1) "Summoning," *ciens;* "but not," *nec;* "cottage:" comp. Hor. *Od.* i. 4. 13, "pauperum *tabernas;*" (2) "company," *coetus;* (3) "only," *non nisi;* "bountiful," *largus.*

IX. (1) "Until," *dum* (with subj.); "remains," *superest;* "kindly," *benignus;* (2) "tricklings," *scatebrae;* "carry away," *defero;* (3) "drain," *haurio.*

EXERCISES XIX, XX

Chorus from the *Alcestis*

Ὦ Πελίου θύγατερ, κ. τ. λ.

EUR. *Alc.* 435, *sqq.*

RETRANSLATION

I

Noble daughter of Pelias, for the last time (2) fare thee well, (thou) *who art bound for* the cruel realms of black Pluto, (3) the black recesses of Erebus (4) devoid of the sun.

II

But let the ruler of the gloomy palace know, (2) and (let him know) who the wan shades (acc.) over the *Stygian river* (3) conveys in his boat, the aged (4) ferryman of Orcus,

III

what a *lady* is approaching his old bark; (2) and with what dutifulness, with what a (3) death illustrious, is she a *noble* spouse for all (4) time.

IV

Yes, but thou shalt live to be long celebrated in song: (2) thee through the vista of years shall *the lyre* rehearse, (3) O Nymph, *deftly* sounding with its seven (4) strings.

V

Or else shall hymns unaccompanied by the lute in *yearly song* (2) tell (of thee), when now, in kindly (3) spring, through the sky the wandering moon with full (4) orb is shining,

VI

what time at Sparta the revolving year *shall bring back* the festival (2) in the Carneian month. Prosperous (3, 4) Athens shall ever sing of thee in hymns and mindful eulogy.

VII

Thy fate (pl.), I trow, yields matter for *glorious* strains. (2) Would that I might now (3) call thee back again to earth, (4) back again to the upper world,

VIII

out of the darksome caverns of Erebus, (2) out of the wave of the gloomy Styx, (and) from the aged (3) waterman's dusky bark, which *ferries over the shades* of the silent.

IX

(As) a wife, the pride of wives dost thou shine unrivalled; (2) who, lavishing thine own life, by a willing (3) death ransomest thy husband *from the palace* of the infernal (4) king.

X

O may the earth lightly cover thy bones: (2) but if thy husband be smitten with a new flame, (3, 4) he will pass the time hated by me, hated by his very children;

XI

seeing that neither his father, stricken in years, nor his aged (2) mother, (though) with hair snow-sprinkled, (3, 4) were willing, instead of their own son, to visit the waters of Acheron.

XII

Yet thou, blooming in early youth, (2) rescuest from death a youthful husband, (3) while by a glorious death thou thyself repairest to black (4) Avernus' shore.

XIII

O may *a bride* excelling in such constancy and dutiful affection (2) fall to my lot: *but* so blessed (3) *a lot* of life have the fates granted to few (4) to draw.

Hints

I. (1) "Noble," *insignis*; "for the last time," *supremum*; (2) "cruel," *ferus*; "Pluto," *Dis* (*-itis*); (3) "art bound for," *petis*; (4) "devoid of," *carens* (with abl.)

II. (1) "Ruler," *moderator*; "palace," *aula*; (2) "over," *per*: (3) "convey," *transveho*; (3) "aged," *senilis*; (4) "ferryman," *portitor*.

III. (1) "Bark," *carina*; (2) "dutifulness," *pietas*; (3) "illustrious," *resplendens*. For the rest comp. Hor. Od. iii. 11. 35, "in omne virgo nobilis aevum."

IV. (1) "Yes, but," *at*; "to be celebrated" (gerundive); "in song," *musis*; (2) "the vista of years," *extenti anni*; "rehearse," *itero*; (3) "lyre," etc.: comp. Hor. Od. iii. 11. 3, "tuque testudo resonare septem callida nervis."

V. (1) "Or else," *aut*; "unaccompanied by," *carens* (as in I. 4); (2) "kindly," *benignus*.

VI. (1) "What time," *ubi*; "revolving," *revolutus*; "festival," *festa* (n. pl.); (2) "the Carneian month" (August), *mensis Carneius*; "prosperous," *beatus*; (3) "eulogy," *laus*.

VII. (1) "I trow," *scilicet*; "yield matter for," *praebeo*; (2) "glorious," *splendidus*; "I might," *liceret*; (3) "upper," *superus*.

VIII. (1) "Darksome," *tenebrosus;* (2) "aged" (see II. 3); (3) "waterman," *nauta;* "dusky," *luridus;* (4) "ferry over," *deveho.*

IX. (1) "Pride," *decus;* "unrivalled," *unus;* (2) "lavish," *fundo;* (3) "ransom," *redimo;* (4 "palace" (see II. 1).

X. (1) "Lightly" (adj.); "thy," *tibi;* (2) "to be smitten," *capi;* (3) "hated by," *invisus* (with dat.) Instead of repeating this word, repeat *ducel.*

XI. (1) "Stricken in years," *annosus;* "nor," *aut;* (2) "snow-sprinkled," *aspersi nivibus* (with acc. of nearer definition).

XII. (1) "Blooming," *viridis;* (2) "rescue," *eximo.*

XIII. (1) "Constancy," *fides;* (2) "fall to the lot of," *contingo* (with dat.); (3) "grant," *tribuo.*

EXERCISE XXI[1]

Telle est la Vie

I

O (thou) who, exulting in golden youth, (2) art seeking uncertain joys, who art attracted by (3) both the unruffled smiles of fortune (4) and the fickle breeze of glittering fame,

II

see how through the unruffled sky (her) lights (2) Aurora sends, while the bark its canvas (3) spreads out, and with a favouring breath (4) the breeze skims over the placid waves;

III

not knowing how dangerous a storm is coming on, (2) with how threatening a burst of the north wind; (3) and with

---

[1] Exercises XXI.-XLVII. are in Alcaic metre. See the Introduction, p. xxix.

(what) black tempest's anger, and (4) with shipwreck balefully charged, the evening is at hand.

IV

So life glides on deceitfully, and fickle (2) fortune changes her winsome smiles: (3) so for each one, ready to mar his pastimes, (4) does the hour of irresistible death press on.

V

For all things *human* yield to pitiless (2) fate; for glory alike (3) and beauty and fortune's gifts (4) are entombed along with the silent urn.

Hints

(1) "Exulting," *laetus*; (2) "who art attracted by" (take the active turn); "whom ... draw," *quem trahunt*, etc.; (3) "unruffled," *serenus*; (4) "fickle," *levis*; "glittering," "brilliant:" comp. Hor. *Sat.* ii. 3. 222, "quem cepit vitrea fama."

II. (1) "Canvas," *carbasa* (n. pl.); (3) "breath," *flatus*; (4) "skim," *volo*.

III. (1) "Not knowing" (referring to "the bark"), *ignara*; "storm," "whirlwind," *turbo*; "burst," *impetus*; (4) "balefully," *male*; "the evening," *vesper* (to begin line 2).

IV. (1) "Deceitfully" (adj.); (2) "winsome," *amabilis*; (3) "ready to mar," *diripio* (fut. part.); comp. Verg. *Aen.* iii. 227 (of the Harpies) "diripiuntque dapes;" (4) "irresistible," *indomitus*; "death," *nex*.

V. (1) "All things (together)" *cuncta*; "pitiless," *inlacrimabilis*; (3) "beauty," *forma*; (4) "entomb," *tumulare*.

EXERCISE XXII

Prometheus Unbound

I

Therefore, sharers of my sufferings, let us *take* (our) way (2) together, where *thick* leaves of woods (3) through the heats of the summer (4) sun, and *where* an ever-flowing *spring* may shed

II

its pleasing coolness around. (2) Here, reclined at ease beneath a grot, we will *look back on* the race (3) of men and the cares of men (4) with influence benign;

III

until, when *kings*, mindful of my chain, (2) have bound their brows with a crown, (3) a sweet *image* of former *sadnesses*, shall steal over (4) our minds.

IV

And thou, O son of supreme Jove, of my (2) preservation the author, what thanks to thee (3) can I pay? But store up in (thy) mind what I prophetically utter to thee.

V

As great as thou wilt leave the grove of the Hesperides, (2) honoured in renown, so great from the lower world (3) wilt thou return, and in safety the triple-headed (4) monster wilt thou lead and bring back to the (upper) air.

VI

A woman alone will conquer thee, a Thessalian (2) mountain (alone); but straightway the starry heights (acc.) (3) shalt thou climb, and enrolled in the peaceful (4) ranks of the gods be among them.

Hints

I. (1) "Sharer," *particeps*; (2) "take," *carpo*; "leaves," *coma*; (3) "heats," *furores*; "of summer" (adj.); (4) "ever-flowing," *inrequietus*.

II. (1) "Spring," *lympha*; "pleasing," *amabilis*; (2) "reclined," *positus*; "at ease," *sic* (lit. "just as we are:" comp. Ter. *Hec.* iv. 1. 11); (3) "of men," *mortalis*; (4) "look back on," "regard," *respicio*: comp. Hor. *Od.* i. 2. 36, "sive neglectum genus ... respicis auctor;" influence," *numen*.

III. (1) "Until," *donec* (with subj.); (3) "sweet" (superl.); "steal over," *obrēpo* (with dat.)

IV. (2) "Preservation," *salus*; (3) "can I pay" (delib. subj.); "store up in," *repono in* (with acc.); (4) "prophetically," *vaticinans*; "utter," *profundo*.

V. (1) "As great as," etc., lit. "With how great fame honoured" (*decorus*); (2) "lower world," "gods below," *inferi*; (3) "triple-headed," lit. "three-tongued," *trilinguis*; (4) "monster," *bēlua*; "wilt lead and bring back," lit. "leading wilt," etc.

VI. (2) Begin with *Te mons*; "starry:" comp. Hor. *Od.* iii. 3. 9, "vagus Hercules enisus arces attigit igneas;" (3) "enrolled in," *adscriptus* (with dat.); (4) "be among," *interesse*.

EXERCISES XXIII, XXIV

Mary Queen of Scots

I

In former days when, confined in ancient towers, (2) the madness (acc. pl.) of her people and the treachery (acc. pl.)

of their leaders (3) the queen was lamenting, on Leven's (4) blue waters gazing,

II

scarce *did she hear* the sound of the lake rippling by (2) and the voices of the balmy air; (3) but (she outdid) the murmur of the waves by her complaint, (4) and by her sighing she outdid the breeze's

III

soft whispers. Beneath the tremulous ray (2) of the moon her uplifted hands (acc.) she piteously (3) stretched forth to the green banks, (4) to the woods and her own realm.

IV

Like as, in the recesses of a wicker dwelling (2) shut up, a captive dove mourns the craft of the husbandmen, (3) at the quiet fields of freedom (4) silently gazing up,

V

(so), terrified by the dreams of the night, (2) she gave the hours of rest to watching, (3) regarding in silent sorrow (4) the disgrace and reproach of the land.

VI

A nation full of unbounded license, (2) with force profane her sovereignty's (3) sceptre and accustomed honours (4) to their lawful mistress had denied,

VII

till she should bewail the useless *years* of youth, (2) the occupant of a lonely prison, (3) and long in sadness for (3,

4) the sacred rites and accustomed worship of her happy home;

VIII

(till she) should long for the brief hours of joy (2) amid the pleasant *vineyards* of fertile France, (3) by the loved shores; (4) her mind retracing a course far distant:

IX

happy, if only under the vine-tendril's shade (2) she were spending a life of innocence, unmindful (3) of grandeur; and, released from care, (4) were recalling the years gone by.

Hints

I. (1) Begin with *Olim ut;* "confined," *conditus;* (2) "leaders," *procĕres;* (3) "Leven's (Lochleven's), *Lĕvĕni;* (4) "gazing on," "watching," *speculata.*

II. (1) "Rippling-by," *obmurmurans;* (4) "sighing," *gemitus.*

III. (1) "Ray," *fax;* (2) "uplifted:" comp. Hor. *Od.* iii. 23. 1, "*caelo supinas si tuleris manus;*" "piteously," *flebiliter;* (4) "woods:" use the resolved form of *silva,* as in Hor. *Od.* i. 23. 4.

IV. (1) "Recesses," *latebrae;* (2) "captive dove," *palumbes* (to end stanza 4, followed by) *captiva;* (3, 4) "gazing up at," *suspiciens* (with acc.)

V. (2) "Watching," *excubiae* (pl.); (3) "regard," *contemplor.*

VI. (1) "Nation," *gens;* "unbounded," *insolens;* (2) "profane:" comp. Hor. *Od.* iii. 6. 10, "non auspicatos contudit inpetus;" (4) "lawful," *legitimus.*

VII. (1) "Till she should," *donec* (with what mood?); "bewail," *fleo;* (2) "lonely," *remotus;* (3) "happy," "prosperous," *beatus;* "worship," *ritus* (pl.)

VIII. (2) "Fertile," *ferax;* (3) "by," *ad;* "loved," *dilectus.*

IX. (1) "If only," *modo* (with what mood?); "vine-tendrils" (adj.), *pampineus;* (2) "of innocence" (adj.); (3) "released from:" comp. Hor. *Od.* iii. 17. 16, "cum famulis operum solutis.'

EXERCISE XXV

Fairest isle, all isles excelling,
    Seat of pleasures and of loves;
Venus here will choose her dwelling,
    And forsake her Cyprian groves.

Cupid from his favourite nation
    Care and envy will remove;
Jealousy that poisons passion,
    And despair that dies for love.

Gentle murmurs, sweet complaining,
    Sighs that blow the fire of love;
Soft repulses, kind disdaining,
    Shall be all the pains you prove.

                              DRYDEN.

RETRANSLATION

I

O isle, loveable beyond all, (2) the seat of loves and of joy, *shady* Cyprus (acc.), (3) on account of thee will Venus (4) forsake; but from his own (pl.) will Cupid

II

take away all bitterness and envy, (2) that none by jealousy, none by lovers' (3) hope deluded, and hating the light, (4) may die. For thee the only care (shall be)

III

sweet complaints, gentle murmurs, (2) sighs that fan the fires of the heart, (3) and *the endearment* of soft disdain and of repulse (4) soon yielding.

HINTS

I. (3) "Venus," Dione; comp. Hor. *Od.* ii. 1. 39, "mecum Dionaeo sub antro;" (4) "his own," *proprii*.

II. (1) "All bitterness," etc.: use *quodcumque* with gen. of the adj. So *quidquid* is used, as in Hor. *Serm.* i. 6. 1, "Lydorum quidquid" (= quicumque Lydi); (2) "jealousy," *livor* (for "jealousy" in its proper sense, as distinguished from "envy" or "malice," no exact equivalent seems to exist in Latin); (3) "deluded," *falsus*; "hating the light:" comp. Verg. *Aen.* vi. 435, "lucemque perosi;" (4) "die," *depereo:* comp. Hor. *Epist.* ii. 1. 40. The transitive use of this word, in the sense of "dote upon," is chiefly in Plautus.

III. (2) "That fan," *alentia*; (3) "repulse:" comp. Hor. *Od.* iii. 2. 19, "virtus *repulsae* nescia sordidae;" (4) "soon yielding:" comp. Hor. *Od.* i. 9. 24, "aut digito male pertinaci." Note this way of expressing a quality by the negation of its opposite; as in Hor. *Serm.* ii. 3. 137, "male tutae mentis Orestes; *ibid.* v. 45, "validus male filius."

EXERCISE XXVI

THE ROSE

The rose had been washed, just washed in a shower,
    Which Mary to Anna conveyed;
The plentiful moisture encumbered the flower,
    And weighed down its beautiful head.

The cup was all filled, and the leaves were all wet,
    And it seemed, to a fanciful view,
To weep for the buds it had left with regret
    On the flourishing bush where it grew.

I hastily seized it, unfit as it was
    For a nosegay, so dripping and drowned;
And swinging it rudely,—too rudely, alas!
    I snapped it: it fell to the ground.

"And such," I exclaimed, "is the pitiless part
    Some act by the delicate mind,
Regardless of wringing and breaking a heart
    Already to sorrow resigned.

This elegant rose, had I shaken it less,
    Might have bloomed with its owner awhile;
And the tear, that is wiped with a little address,
    May be followed, perhaps, by a smile."

COWPER.

RETRANSLATION

I

Sprinkled (acc.) with the dews of recent showers, (2) Maria brought a rose, a sweet gift (3) to Anna; but the dripping *moisture* was weighing down (4) its dainty head, a heavy burden.

II

And so wet was the cup with raindrops, (2) so much water was hidden beneath the leaves, (3, 4) that you would have almost believed it to be weeping in sorrow for the flowers left behind.

III

I hastily seized (it), as a fitting gift (2) which I might

place amid the garlands of flowers, (3) and shook it (when) seized; but alas! (4) it lay a broken ruin on the ground.

IV

"Thus, at times," I said, "grieving hearts (acc.) (2) do pitiless-ones harass with lashes, (3) heedless of crushing (them), with pain (4) long weighed-down and with heavy cares.

V

"This beautiful flower, had it not, by eager hand (2) seized, perished, perchance this bosom (acc.) (3) might have been adorning: *so* kindly wiped-away (4) tears (acc.) do joys follow."

Hints

I. (2) Maria—Anna. These names may be left unchanged, or others of equivalent quantity chosen, as Corinna, Ida; (3) "Dripping," *effusus*.

II. (1) "So wet was," *tantum* . . . *immaduit*. (3) "In sorrow," *maerentem*.

III. (2) "Place," *repono* (imp. subj.)

IV. (3) "Heedless of," *incautus*, with inf.; crush, "*profligo*."

V. (1) "Had it not," *ni* (a word found once in the Epodes of Horace, but not in the Odes).

EXERCISES XXVII, XXVIII

The Parrot

In painted plumes superbly drest,
A native of the gorgeous east,
 By many a billow tost;

Poll gains at length the British shore,
Part of the captain's precious store,
   A present to his toast.

Belinda's maids are soon preferr'd
To teach him now and then a word,
   As Poll can master it;
But 'tis her own important charge
To qualify him more at large,
   And make him quite a wit.

Sweet Poll! his doating mistress cries,
Sweet Poll! the mimic bird replies,
   And calls aloud for sack;
She next instructs him in the kiss,
'Tis now a little one like Miss,
   And now a hearty smack.

At first he aims at what he hears,
And listening close with both his ears
   Just catches at the sound;
But soon articulates aloud,
Much to th' amusement of the crowd,
   And stuns the neighbours round.

COWPER.

RETRANSLATION

1.

With plumage painted in proud colours, (2) borne through *the waves* of the swelling sea, (3) setting forth from the East, (1) a parrot approaches the English shores, a good part of the rich cargo, (2) which the captain is eagerly *hastening* to his (3) maid to present, (4) a costly pet.

III

She determines to consign (it) to-be-trained (2) to servants, that it may *be taught* a few (3) rudiments of speech, (4) (being) apt to repeat new sounds.

IV

This important function *Belinda* herself discharges, (2) that, rendered more talkative by practice, (3) it may further-learn unaccustomed graces (4) and repeat tender complaints.

V

If she chooses to say first "How do you do?" a second (2) "How do you do?" rejoins the parrot with rival (3) cry; then *it bids* the attendants wine (acc.) (4) to bring, and calls for glasses.

VI

Soon, not unskilled in kissing, she teaches (it) (2) to taste with its beak the kisses of loving ones, (3) now like an unwilling maid, (4) now redoubled (n. pl.) with an eager smack.

VII

At first delighting to take-in what it hears, (2) soon with attentive ears it drinks-in (3) whatever of whispered gossip (4) the breeze may waft through slender chinks.

VIII

Soon it repeats it with bolder tone, (2) while the neighbourhood rings with applause, (3) and the wondering crowds laugh at (4) the novel scoldings of so teachable a tongue.

Hints

I. (1) "With plumage" (acc. of respect); (2) "swelling," *tumultuosus*; (4.) "English," *Angliacus*, or *occiduus*.

II. (1) "Cargo," *sarcina*; (2) "captain," lit. "master of the ship;" (4) "pet," *deliciae*. For the form of the line comp. Hor. *Od.* iii. 1. 48, *Divitias operosiores*.

III. (2) "A few," *unum . . . et alterum*; (3) "rudiments" (sing.).

IV. (1) "Important," *magnus*; (3) "further learn," *addisco*.

V. (1) "To say first," *praeire verbis*, a phrase used of dictating the terms of an oath, etc., to another, who was said *jurare in verba*; (2) "rejoin," *repono*; (3) "cry," *clamor*; (4) "glass," *cyathus*.

VI. (3) "Like," *more* (c. genit.); "unwilling," *nolens*; "smack," *plausus*.

VII. (1) "To take in," *duco*; (2) "attentive," *adplicatus*.

VIII. (1) "Tone," *sonus*; (2) "neighbourhood," *vicina . . . loca*; (4) "scoldings," *probrum* (pl.)

EXERCISE XXIX

Alexander's Feast

Soothed with the sound, the king grew vain;
Fought all his battles o'er again;
And thrice he routed all his foes, and thrice he slew the slain.
The master saw the madness rise,
His glowing cheeks, his ardent eyes;

And, while he heav'n and earth defied,
Chang'd his hand, and checked his pride.
  He chose a mournful muse,
  Soft pity to infuse;
He sung Darius great and good,
  By too severe a fate
Fallen, fallen, fallen, fallen,
Fallen from his high estate,
  And welt'ring in his blood;
Deserted, at his utmost need,
By those his former bounty fed:
On the bare earth expos'd he lies,
With not a friend to close his eyes.
       DRYDEN.

RETRANSLATION

I

The king, touched at heart by the pleasing strain (2) was growing vain: renewing his wars (3) (already) fought, the vanquished cohorts (acc.) (4) he thrice routed, and the slain with triple

II

blow he slew. Not without the *master's* observing it (2) glares the darting *flash* of his eyes, (3) and, as his countenance reddens, (4) fierce anger has exasperated his soul.

III

Nay, he challenges to impious contests (2) the earth and the powers of the gods; when the (master's) hand,

(3, 4) changing, *abates* the proud tumults of his breast (now) curbed.

IV.

See! with mournful strain he has skilfully (2) soothed his anger (pl.): Fallen, fallen (3) has Darius undeservedly, and in his own (4) blood is weltering, unworthy (of such a fate).

V.

They whom his bounteous hand had formerly enriched (2) leave (him) destitute in his last hour; (3) and of him lying beneath the void expanse, (4) the eyes (acc.) no dutiful hand closes.

HINTS

I. (1) "At heart" (acc. of respect); "pleasing," *amabilis*; (2) "renewing," *redintegrans*.

II. (1) "Not without," etc., *non sine conscio . . . magistro*; (2) "darting," *tortilis*; "eyes," *orbes*; (3) "and as," etc., lit. "to him reddening as to his countenance" (acc. pl.)

III. (3) "Changing," *mutata*; "curbed," *frenati*; (4) "abates," *inminuit*.

IV. (2) "Has fallen," *occidit*; (4) "is weltering," *volvitur*.

V. (2) "Hour," *tempus*; (3) "void expanse," *vasto . . . diro*; (4) "no," *non*.

EXERCISES XXX, XXXI

Come, sweet harp, resounding
Teian strains of yore,
With soft airs abounding
Round the Lesbian shore;
Doric shell, awake thy soft strains no more.

Talk no more of maiden
    Fair with beauty's wiles,
Youth with blessings laden
    Whom new life beguiles,
Smiling as it flies, flying as it smiles.

Wisdom which ne'er wrongeth,
    Born of God above,
Toils in birth, and longeth
    Your sweet chords to prove,
And hath bid me flee woes of earthly love.

What is strength, or glory,
    Beauty, gold, or fame,
What renown in story,
    Or a kingly name,
To the thoughts of God—cares which bring not blame?

One o'er steeds is bending,
    One his bow hath strung,
One his gold is tending,
    One by youth is sung
For bright looks, and locks o'er his shoulders hung.

Mine be the low portal,
    Paths in silence trod,
Knowing not things mortal,
    Knowing things of God;
While still at my side Wisdom holds her rod.

        SYNESIUS, Ode I.
  (Translated in the *British Magazine*, 1841.)

RETRANSLATION

I

O lute, that didst resound, by Teian (2) thumb erst struck, *hard by* the Lesbian (3) shore, and wert wont around (4) to reiterate thy sweet-voiced strains;

II

cease at length from soft measures, (2) nor let there delay thee the virgin's wily (3) beauty, O Dorian lyre, (4) nor the youth laden with every

III

splendour of life, whom, credulous-one, new (2) time-of-life now beguiles, but soon passes-by, (3) ready-to-mock (him) with laughter. Now a changed (4) melody pour forth. Wisdom,

IV

offspring of God, that knows no guile, (2) is travailing with a fresh birth; now she hastens the chords (3) to try, and of earthly love (4) the grief (acc.) has forbidden me to sing.

V

What avails strength, or what glory, what (2) gold, or maiden's beauty, what honour, (3) and a name adorned by the muses (4), what the ancestry and titles of kings?

VI

Me let the care of God on high detain, (2) (a care) to-be-blamed by none. One is absorbed, on golden (3) hoards intent; another *youth* in high-spirited (4) steed delights; a third is bending

VII

the bow: another the sportive bands of youths (2) praise, and his locks (acc.) floating from his shoulder, (3) and his fair countenance; but the lowly portal be it lawful for me to enter,

VIII

and let Wisdom guide me with (her) rod; that spots (2) trodden in silence I may safely traverse, (3) and released from mortal care (4) may strive to know the behests of God.

HINTS

I. (1) "Teian," *Teio* (‿‿), Teos being the birth-place of Anacreon. Hence Hor. *Od.* i. 17. 18, *fide Teia;* (3) "hard by," *ad;* (4) "sweet-voiced," *dulciloquus*.

II. (1) "Cease from:" comp. Hor. *Od.* ii. 9. 17, "desine mollium tandem querelarum;" (4) "nor," *neve;* "laden," *cumulatus*.

III. (2) "But," *at;* "soon," *brevi:* comp. Ov. *Met.* v. 32; (3) "ready to mock," *lusura;* "changed," *novatum;* (4) "Wisdom," *Sophia*, a word which suits the Greek character of the piece; personified in later times as the Divine Wisdom. Comp. Ennius, "nec quisquam sophiam, sapientia quae perhibetur, in somnis vidit;" and Mart. *Epigr.* i. 112. 1. The word for "with fresh" (*inf.* IV. 2) comes at the end of this line.

IV. (1) "That knows no guile:" comp. Hor. *Od.* i. 6. 6 "Pelidae... cedere nescii;" (2) "fresh" (see note on III. 4); "chords," *fides;* (4) "to sing," *celebrare*.

V. (1) "Avails" (last word in line); (2) "beauty," *gratia;* (4) "ancestry:" comp. Juv. *Sat.* viii. 1, "Stemmata quid prosunt?"

VI. (1) "On high," *summi;* (2) "by none" (case after gerundive?). "One," "another," etc.; a variety of words may be used, as *pars, hic, ille, est qui* (or *quem*). Comp. Verg. *Aen.* ii. 31, "pars stupet innuptae donum exitiale Minervae," and Hor. *Od.* i. 1. 3, 7, 9; (3) "high-spirited," *ferox*.

VII. (2) "Floating," *natantes;* (3) "countenance," *voltus* (pl.); "lowly," *modestus;* (4) "to enter," *subiisse*.

VIII. (4) "To know," *nosse;* "behests," *monitus* (pl.).

EXERCISES XXXII, XXXIII

Hymn of Pan

From the forests and highlands
    We come, we come;
From the river-girt islands
    Where loud waves are dumb
        Listening to my sweet pipings.
The wind in the reeds and the rushes,
    The bees on the bells of thyme,
The birds in the myrtle-bushes,
    The cicale above in the lime,
And the lizards below in the grass,
Were as silent as ever old Tmolus was,
        Listening to my sweet pipings.

Liquid Peneus was flowing,
    And all dark Tempe lay
In Pelion's shadow, outgrowing
    The light of the dying day,
        Speeded by my sweet pipings.
The Sileni and Sylvans and Fauns,
    And the Nymphs of the woods and waves,
To the edge of the moist river-lawns
    And the brink of the dewy caves,
And all that did then attend and follow,
Were silent with love, as you now, Apollo,
        With envy of my sweet pipings.
                  SHELLEY.

RETRANSLATION

I

I am come, nor do the shades nor mountain grots (2) nor islands skirted by streams (3) detain (me), now that the lulled *waves* from their roaring (4) have subsided, by the sweet

II

hum of my pipe lulled. (2) Neither the wind among the wet reeds; (3) nor the lizard hidden in a covert of (4) turf, nor the cicales clinging to the

III

lime-tree top, nor the thyme-plants by the bees (2) deflowered, nor the flock of birds (3) perched on the myrtle-bushes, made a noise; (4) vanquished by the strains of my pipe;

IV

at which soothing music Tmolus was hushed, (2) listening in days gone by. In sooth with watery (3) stream Peneus was flowing (4) crystal-clear, and Tempe (acc.) with its coverts

V

Pelion was filling with shade, on to the dark (2) valleys swiftly settling down, (3) at the fall of the declining day, (4) the sweet-toned breathing of my reed

VI

hastening (it): but thither, along with wayward (2) Fauns,

bands of Satyrs with pricked-up ears, and (3) Silenus, and whatever *goddesses love* the springs, (4) whatever the woods,

VII

came; whether on the dewy marge (2) of a cave they were standing, or by rivulets (3) laving the green sward; but them (4) sweet love kept in my train,

VIII

and locked their bosoms in deep silence. (2) But thou, Phœbus, art speechless now with envy: (3) thee jealousy hath o'ermastered, (4) hearing the sweet-toned melody of my pipe.

Hints

I. (1) "I am come," *adsum;* "mountain grots," *cava montium;* "skirted," *praenatatus:* comp. Verg. Aen. vi. 705; "stream," *fons;* (3) "now that," *ut;* "roaring," *planctus:* comp. Lucr. vi. 690; (4) "subside," *detumesco.*

II. (1) "Pipe," *fistula,* and (later on) *cicūta;* (3) "in a covert of turf," *inducto cespite;* (4) "cicales," or tree-crickets: comp. Verg. Ecl. ii. 13, "resonant arbusta *cicadis;*" "clinging to," *forentes.*

III. (1) "Top" (use *summus* in agr. with its noun); "thyme-plants:" comp. Hor. Od. iv. 2. 29, "apis . . . grata carpentis *thyma;*" (2) "deflowered," *depasta florem;* "flock," *cohors;* (3) "perched," *suspensa;* (4) "strains," *modulis.*

IV. (1) "At which . . . music," *quod . . . ad melos;* "was hushed" (use historic pres.); (2) "listening," "with ears pricked up:" comp. Hor. Od. i. 12. 11, "*auritas* . . . ducere quercus;" "in days gone by," *olim;* (3) "stream," *fluentum;* "Peneus:" see note on Ex. LV. ii. 4 below; (4) "with its coverts," *late-brosa* (n. pl.).

V. (2) "Settling down," *cadente . . . desuper;* (3) "declining," *vergens.*

VI. (1) "Hastening," *citante* (abl. abs.); "along with," *non sine;* "wayward," *devius;* (2) 'Satyrs:" comp. Hor. Od. ii. 19. 4, "aures Capripedum Satyrorum acutas." Hence *acuti Capripedum chori* may be used here ; (3) "whatever," *quidquid*, with gen. ; "springs," *scatebrae* ; (4) "woods :" comp. Hor. *Od.* i. 23. 4, "aurarum et *siluae* metu."

VII. (3) "Laving," *lambentes :* comp. Hor. *Od.* i. 22. 8 ; "greensward," *virectum* (pl.) ; (4) "in my train," lit. "following."

VIII. (1) "Locked," *clausit* ; "bosoms," *corda* ; (3) "jealousy," *livor ;* (4) "pipe" (to come at end of line 3).

EXERCISE XXXIV

Go up and watch the new-born rill
    Just trickling from its mossy bed,
Streaking the heath-clad hill
    With a bright emerald thread.

Canst thou her bold career foretell,
    What rocks she shall o'erleap or rend,
How far in ocean's swell
    Her freshening billows send ?

Perchance that little brook shall flow
    The bulwark of some mighty realm,
Bear navies to and fro,
    With monarchs at their helm.

Or canst thou guess how far away
    Some sister nymph, beside her urn
Reclining night and day,
    'Mid reeds and mountain fern,

Nurses her store, with thine to blend,
    When many a moor and glen are past,
Then in the wide sea end
    Their spotless lives at last ?

KEBLE.

Retranslation

I

Go where, now bickering with new bubblings (2) from its bed green with moss, steals-forth (3) the rivulet, and marks with a shining (4) and glassy *streak* the purple hills:

II

is it granted to thee as yet to forecast (2) what rocks it may soon with strong course from above (3) sweep (away) or rend? *how far* its waves (4) into the roaring sea

III

it may send (now) swollen? In sooth its (2) waters may delight dread (3) fleets (acc.) and kings as admirals (4) to bear, the pride and support of the land.

IV

Canst thou perchance believe, how, far hence a sister (2) nymph amid the reeds and holm-oaks this (rivulet) (3) awaits, and reclining by her urn (4) by night and day with stores her twin

V

stream nourishes, till thine has finished (2) its course through meads, through woods; and the two (3) may lay down at-the-entrance-of the boundless *ocean* (their) living (4) waters without spot.

Hints

I. (1) "Bickering:" comp. Hor. *Od.* ii. 3. 12, "laborat lympha fugax *trepidare* rivo;" (2) "shining," *renidens*.

II. (1) "Streak," *sulcus*; "forecast," *augurari*; "course," *pede*; (3) "sweep," *verro*; the enclitic *ve* is to be joined to each verb; (4) "roaring sea," *strepitus marinus*.

III. (1) "Swollen," *auctos* (agr. with *fluctus*); (2) "may:" comp. Hor. *Od.* iii. 1. 9, "*est ut* viro vir latius ordinet*," etc.; (3) "as admirals," *custodes*; (4) "support," *columen*.

IV. (1) "Canst thou perchance," *an forte*; (3) "reclining by," *acclinis ad*; (4) "stores," *opes*.

V. (1) "Thine," *tuus* (sc. *amnis*); "finish," *haurio*; (3) "lay down," *remitto*; "at the entrance of," *sub* (acc.)

EXERCISES XXXV, XXXVI

Know ye not that lovely river?
Know ye not that smiling river,
Whose gentle flood by cliff and wood
With wildering sound goes wandering ever?

O often yet with feeling strong
On that dear stream my memory ponders;
And still I prize its murmuring song;
For by my childhood's home it wanders.

There's music in each wind that blows,
Around our native valley breathing;
There's beauty in each flower that grows,
Around our native woodland wreathing.

The memory of the lightest joys
In childhood's happy morn that found us,
Is dearer than the richest toys
The present vainly sheds around us.

O sister, when with doubts and fears
That haunt life's onward journey ever,
I turn to those departed years
And that beloved and lovely river,

My sinking heart with suffering riven,
And soul with lonely anguish aching,—
It needs my long-taught hope in heaven
To keep that weary heart from breaking.

Retranslation

I

Knowest thou the charms of my rivulet? (2) Knowest thou its smiles? with gentle waters it (3) wanders through rocks, through woods, (4) ever-repeating its soothing murmurs.

II

Oh! often, with too mindful plaint, thee (2) have I regretted, beloved river, (3) that utterest a murmuring song, (4) a stream dear to me beyond others.

III

Outside the door of my childhood's cottage (2) do not the breezes more sweetly (3) blow in my native vale? (4) Blooms there not through ancestral woodlands

IV

a more pleasing beauty of flowers? Oh! to me (2) if the glad light were to rise again, in *happy* childhood (3) which first smiled, (4) soon the more troublesome offerings (acc.)

V

would I readily resign, all that the fleeting hour (2) has lavished upon me disdaining (them). (3) But amid the uncertain honours, (4) dear sister, with which at all times the painful

VI

path of life is hampered, *if it chance that to* the clear (2) windings of my beloved river (3) and the years gone by I return, (4) when distracting anguish *torments my lonely* breast,

VII

and my mind with *extremest* pains (2) is sinking,—what but *a sure hope* of portals (3) celestial refreshes (4) my heart, riven with its own remorse?

Hints

I. (1) "Charms," *deliciae;* "rivulet," *rivus;* (4) "soothing," *blandiloquus;* "murmurs," *susurri.*

II. (2) "Beloved, *amabile;* (3) "utter," *educo;* "murmuring song," lit. "musical (*canorum*) murmur;" (4) "stream;" *lympha.*

III. (1) "Cottage," *villula:* comp. also Hor. *Od.* iii. 4. 10, "altricis extra limen," etc.; (2) "breezes," *Favonii;* comp. Introd. p. xlviii; "more sweetly," *mellitiores;* (4) "woodlands," "wilds," *tesqua.*

IV. (2) "Were to" (pres. subj.); (3) "smile," *subrideo;* (4) "more troublesome:" comp. Hor. *Od.* iii. 1. 48, "divitias operosiores."

V. (1) "Readily," "without waiting to be asked," *ultro;* comp. also Hor. *Od.* iii. 29. 54, "resigno quae dedit;" "all that," *quanta . . . cumque* (in different lines); (2) "has lavished upon," *profundo* (pft. subj., with dative); (4) "painful," *aegra.*

VI. (1) "Hamper," *impedio;* (2) "if it chance that," *si forte* (in line 2); (3) "gone by," *delapsi;* (4) "distracting," *male sanus.*

VII. (1) "Lonely," *desertus;* (2) "is sinking," *languet;* (3) "refreshes," *refecit,* usitative aorist; (4) "remorse," *morsus.*

EXERCISES XXXVII, XXXVIII

*   *   *   *

You first I call on, brothers o'er the sea,
   Swarm from the hive of England's populous shore,
Who with strong purpose struggled to be free,
   And now can own a foreign yoke no more.
      A hundred years are fled
      Since your uplifted head
In freedom shook its tresses to the sun:
      Well may ye celebrate
      With civic pomp and state
The day that saw your federal life begun.

Ye too, the lusty sons of later time,
   Canadian, or Australian, or where'er
Your foot is planted in obscurer clime,
   Freedom still loving unconfined as air;
      Linked by the common tie
      Of English ancestry,
Close round the hearth of your old island home:
      In spirit close around,
      And let your hearts rebound
Responsive to the call that bids you come.

J. H. L.

15th September 1887.

RETRANSLATION

I

(You) first will I summon, who have a home *across the*

deep seas, (2) brotherly hearts, from *crowded* Britain (3) a swarm sent forth, (4) a brood strong of purpose,

II

hearts devoted to a lot of freedom, (2) and ready with an effort to burst the bonds, (3, 4) and not over patient in bearing the ancient law of a foreign king.

III

Now the hundredth year is passing, (2) since (your) nation in freedom *uplifted* (its) proud head, (3) and shook-out its tresses (4) to the sunbeams and the bright sky :

IV

therefore will it be fitting to pour forth strains, (2) and duly to lead the civic procession : (3, 4) this was the first day that gave to your compacts a duly ratified honour.

V

You next, as many as a later age has brought forth, (2) Australians, or Canadians, I call on ; (3, 4) or whatever land less known in situation the settlers (acc.) of our race

VI

has ever welcomed, stout hearts, (2) in whom, even though distant, the old love remains (3) implanted, and the heart's desire (4) more free than the zephyr's breath ;

VII

whom one unbroken tie holds bound together, (2) and a

name derived from British stock; (3) guard ye the fire and the hearth (4) that our island has made and makes its home;

VIII

guard firm faith with souls united. (2) So let *that voice* throbbingly rouse the hearts of all, (3, 4) which has summoned its scattered offspring to return to their native land.

HINTS

I. (1) "Summon," *cieo*; "who have," lit. "to whom (there is);" "sea," *aequor*; (2) "brotherly hearts," *fratrum corda*; (3) "swarm:" comp. Hor. *Od.* I. 35. 30, "iuvenum recens examen;" "crowded," *frequens*; (4) "strong of purpose:" comp. Hor. *Od.* iii. 3. 1, "iustum et tenacem propositi virum."

II. (1) "Of freedom" (adj.); (2) "ready," *promptus* (with inf.); "with an effort," *nisu*; (3) "ancient," "of bygone days," *vetustus*; "over patient," *tam dociles* (with inf.: comp. Hor. *Od.* i. 1. 18, indocilis pauperiem pati").

III. (1) "Is passing," lit. "is spending its days," *agit dies*; (2) "since," *ex quo (tempore)*; "in freedom" (adj.); (3) "tresses," *crines*.

IV. (2) "Procession," *pompa*; (3) "this was the first . . . that," *haec prima*; (4) "duly ratified," "consecrated," *auspicatus*.

V. (1) "You next," *tum vos*; (2) "Australians, Canadians," *Australienses, Canadae*; (3) "whatever," *si qua*; "of our race," *nostrates*; (4) "in situation," *regione*.

VI. (1) "Welcome," *excipio*; (2) "even though," *et*; "old," *priscus*; (3) "desire," *voluntas*; (4) "breath," *susurrus*.

VII. (1) "Unbroken tie," "uniform course," *tenor*: comp. Verg. *Georg.* ii. 337; (2) "derived from," *ortum* (with abl.); (3) "hearth," *lares*; (4) "has made and makes its home," *coluit coluitque*: comp. Hor. *Od.* ii. 13. 20, "vis rapuit rapietque gentes."

VIII. (1) "Souls," *animi*; (2) "throbbingly," *pulsans*: comp. Verg. *Aen.* v. 138, "exsultantiaque haurit corda pavor pulsans;" (3) "scattered," *sparsus*; (4) "summon," *cieo*.

EXERCISES XXXIX, XL, XLI

Ode

I

Welcome, welcome with one voice!
In your welfare we rejoice,
Sons and brothers, that have sent
From isle and cape and continent
Produce of your field and flood,
Mount, and mine, and primal wood,
Works of subtle brain and hand,
And splendours of the Morning Land,
Gifts from every British zone!
    Britons, hold your own!

II

May we find, as ages run,
The mother featured in the son,
And may yours for ever be
That old strength and constancy
Which has made your fathers great
In our ancient island state!
 And, where'er her flag may fly
Glorying between sea and sky,
Make the might of Britain known!
    Britons, hold your own!

III

Britain fought her sons of yore,
Britain failed; and never more,

Careless of our growing kin,
Shall we sin our fathers' sin:
Men that in a narrower day—
Unprophetic rulers they—
Drove from out the Mother's nest
That young eagle of the West,
To forage for herself alone!
    Britons, hold your own!

IV

Sharers of our glorious past,
Brothers, must we part at last?
Shall we not thro' good and ill
Cleave to one another still?
Britain's myriad voices call:
Sons be welded, each and all,
Into one Imperial whole;
One with Britain, heart and soul!
One life, one flag, one fleet, one Throne!
    Britons, hold your own!
    And God guard all!

TENNYSON.

From *The Times*, 5th May 1886.

RETRANSLATION

I

Hail, brothers! this (acc.) the *voice* of all together (2) congratulating (you) safe-and-well bids: (3) hail, ye sons, *whom* with distant (4) cliffs an island, or the sea

II

divides from well-nigh the whole world. Hither dutifully (2) whatever is swept from native threshing-floors, (3) whatever (acc.) the mountain and the unexplored forests, (4) whatever (acc.) the lake or the mine has,

III

ye readily pay (as) tribute. Lo! *how much the strength* of hand (2) and intellect works out; (3) and *how great gifts* the nations attached to Britons (4) bring, *blended* with an eastern shore's

IV

sparkling jewels. (2) Do ye, my countrymen, duly guard what has been won; (3) so that through the gliding years a late (4) progeny may recall its sire.

V

Yours be, as of old, strengthening the heart, (2) the valour, in which the race of your forefathers was strong, (3) while our citadel, with a belt of the encompassing (4) sea encircled, remained unshaken.

VI

Striving in this spirit, *wherever* (our) soldier to the air (2) proudly uplifts the standards, (3) to be waved betwixt sea and sky, (4) he teaches the unconquerable might of Britons.

VII

In an ill-omened *encounter* did England with its children (2) once join in war, (3) infatuate! but to repeat the shocking (4) wrong, like (our) fathers, it refuses,

VIII

forgetful of (its) offspring. With its leaders, in an *evil* day, that race ignorantly drove forth (3) from its parent nest (one) struggling in resistance, (4) to *seek for* its food, like the bird of Jove,

IX

alone on Atlantic shores. (2) Brothers, with whom not ingloriously (3) we have encountered, shall we be parted? (4) How much better, bound in natural affection,

X

to bear whatever is to be borne! (2) Listen to the countless voices of those admonishing us: (3) "Divided brood of children, (4) continue ye in one empire."

XI

So to the peoples shall be a life in harmony, so (2) (shall be) one warfare, one love tending the throne: (3) so let Britons protect what they have won, (4) and do thou, O God, guard all.

HINTS

I. (1) "Together," *simul;* (2) "congratulate," *grātulari* (with dat.); "safe and well," *sospĕs, -ĭtis;* (4) "cliff," *scopulus.*

II. (1) "Dutifully" (adj.), *pius;* (2) "whatever," etc.: comp. Hor. *Od.* i. 1. 10, "quidquid de Libycis verritur areis;" (3) "unexplored," *intactus;* (4) "mine," *metallum.*

III. (1) "Readily," *ultro;* (2) "strength," *robur;* "intellect," *ingenium;* (3) "attached:" comp. Hor. *Od.* iii. 5. 3, "adiectis Britannis imperio;" (4) "how great gifts," *quanta* (in III. 4) *dona* (in IV. 1).

IV. (1) "Blended," *commixtus;* (2) "my countrymen," *cives;* "guard," *tueor,* "what has been won," *partus* (n. pl.); (4) "recall," *referre.*

V. (1) "Strengthening:" comp. Hor. *Od.* iv. 4. 34, "rectique cultus pectora roborant;" (2) "of your forefathers," *avitus;* (3) "belt,' *zona;* "encircling," *refusus:* comp. Verg. *Aen.* vii. 225, "si quem tellus extrema refuso submovet oceano;" (4) "unshaken," *stabilis.*

VI. (1) "In this spirit:" comp. Hor. *Od.* iii. 3. 9, "hac arte . . . enisus;" (2) "proudly," *superbiens;* (3) "wave," *vibro.*

VII. (1) "Ill-omened," *non auspicatus;* "join in encounter," *manus consero;* (2) "war," *duellum;* "shocking," *infandus;* (4) "like our fathers," *more patrum.*

VIII. (2) "Evil," *iniquus;* "ignorantly" (adj.), *inscius:* comp. Hor. *Od.* iv. 4. 6, 11, "nido laborum propulit inscium . . . nunc in reluctantes dracones egit amor dapis," etc.; (4) "to seek for," *qui* (in VIII. 4) *captaret* (in IX. 1).

IX. (1) "Atlantic," *Atlanticus:* comp. Hor. *Od.* i. 31. 14, "not ingloriously," *non sine gloria;* (3) "we have encountered," *res gesta (est);* "shall we be," *licebit;* (4) "how much better," etc.: comp. Hor. *Od.* i. 11. 3: "ut melius quidquid erit pati;" (4) "natural affection," *pietas.*

X. (2) "Of those admonishing us," *monentium* (to come in X. 1); (3) "brood," *propago;* (4) "combine," *coco.*

XI. (1) "In harmony," *concors;* (2) "warfare," *mars;* "tend," *colo;* "throne," *sceptrum* (pl.); (3) "protect," *defendo;* (4) "guard," (pres. subj.) See above, IV. 2.

EXERCISE XLII

Cyriack, whose grandsire on the royal bench
   Of British Themis, with no mean applause,
   Pronounc'd, and in his volumes taught, our laws,
Which others at the bar so often wrench,
To-day deep thoughts resolve with me to drench
   In mirth that after no repenting draws.
   Let Euclid rest and Archimedes pause,
And what the Swede intend, and what the French.

To measure life learn thou betimes, and know
  Toward solid good what leads the nearest way:
  For other things mild Heav'n a time ordains,
And disapproves that care, though wise in show,
  That with superfluous burden loads the day,
  And, when God sends a cheerful hour, refrains.

MILTON.

RETRANSLATION

I

O illustrious offspring of an illustrious grandsire, (2) who, the glory of our court, *apportioned* laws (3) to Britons with praise (4) not slender, and taught (them) *prudently* in (his) books

II

to keep honour, by crooked pleaders (2) distorted; drinking with me to-day, (3, 4) let go weightier matters, Dellius, in an enjoyment we need not blush at.

III

For a little while let Archimedes and the sage of Phãros (2) be laid aside, though thou longest to unfold their writings; (3) forbear to be anxious as to what *Teutonic* nations threaten, (4) and the discordant Rhone.

IV

Do thou remember betimes *to arrange in just measure* the present life, (2) and (remember) what is the shortest (3) *way* of virtue that *leads* to heaven. (4) God has ordained

V

the rest, with foreknowledge of the future ; nor approves (2) if one with scanty wisdom *allots* the day to *disproportionate* toil, (4) and *spares* to enjoy (4) a time of greater freedom.

HINTS

I. (1) "Offspring," *progenies;* (2) "court," *cūria;* "laws," *jura;* (3) "apportion," *divido;* (4) "books," *chartae;* "prudently" (in II. 1), adj.

II. (1) "Honour," *honestum; honor* would mean "a distinction," "honourable office;" "crooked pleaders," *prava loquentes;* (3, 4) "weightier matters" (n. pl. of comp. adj.) ; "Dellius" (for the choice of this name, comp. Hor. Od. ii. 3); "we need not blush at," *non erubescendus.*

III. (1) "Sage," *senex;* (who is referred to ?) (2) "be laid aside, though," etc., lit. "be wanting to (thee) longing," *aventi;* (3) "forbear:" comp. Hor. Od. iii. 29. 11, "omitte mirari ;" the ode throughout will illustrate this sonnet of Milton, as also, in part, will ode i. 9 ; "to be anxious," *curare*, to begin IV. (1).

IV. (1) "Remember," *memento,* to come at end of line 3 ; "the present life," *vitae . . . quod adest:* comp. Hor. Od. iii. 29. 32, "quod adest memento componere aequus ;" (2) "what is . . . that," lit. "and what shortest . . . leads."

V. (1) "With foreknowledge of," etc.: comp. Hor. Od. iii. 29. 29 ; "approves," *favet;* (2) "with scanty wisdom," *vix sapiens;* (3) *disproportionate, iniustus;* (4) "of greater freedom" (comp. adj.)

EXERCISE XLIII

That there's a self, which after death shall live,
All are concern'd about and all believe ;
That something's ours, when we from life depart,
This all conceive, all feel it at the heart:
The wise of learn'd antiquity proclaim

This truth, the public voice declares the same :
No land so rude, but looks beyond the tomb
For future prospects in a world to come.
Hence, without hopes to be in life repaid,
We plant slow oaks, posterity to shade ;
And hence vast pyramids, aspiring high,
Lift their proud heads aloft and time defy.
Hence is our love of fame ; a love so strong,
We think no dangers great, or labours long,
By which we hope our beings to extend,
And to remotest times in glory to descend.

S. JENYNS.

RETRANSLATION

I

Death has not strength to destroy all of us, (2) and a surviving part (acc.) of himself each one (3) will save from Orcus ; nor all (4) (our) life (acc.) does ruthless Lĭbĭtina seize.

II

This does the mind of all care for, this *faith* does it conceive (2) stored up in the depths of the heart ; (3) this of old did *learned* Greece maintain ; (4) the voice of the thronging people

III

unanimously proclaims this ; this does the Scythian (2) and the Indian from remotest shores believe, (3) and looks forward to happy plains (4) designed for himself after the grave.

IV

In truth (it is) in this hope of a hereafter (that) *a man plants trees*, (2) unmindful of present use, (3) and arranges a slow-growing shade (4) to be enjoyed not by himself but by posterity.

V

Hence the foundation of royal pyramids (2) upbears (their) summits raised on high, (3) and haughty piles repel (4) the destruction of time as it flies.

VI

Hence fame distracts with passionate longing (2) (men) prepared both to do and to suffer anything whatever, (3) in order that for them, destined to live to distant ages, (4) (their) descendants may celebrate (their) honour.

Hints

I. (1) "All of us," *i.e.* "the whole of our being," *omne nostrum:* comp. Hor. *Od.* iii. 30. 6.

II. (1) "This does," etc; begin with *Hoc curat;* (2) "stored up:" comp. Verg. *Aen.* i. 26; "heart," *pectora;* (3) "maintain," *confirmo;* (4) "thronging," *frequens.*

III. (1) "Unanimously," *consentiens;* (3) "look forward to," *prospecto* (with acc.); (4) "grave," *tumulus;* "designed," *destinatus.*

IV. (1) "A hereafter," *futurum;* "a man," *vir* (to come in line 3): comp. Hor. *Od.* iii. 1. 9; "plants," *conserit* (in line 2); (3) "arrange," *dispono;* "slow-growing," lit. "coming late," *serus;* (4) "posterity," *suboles.*

V. (1) Comp. Hor. *Od.* iii. 30. 2, "*regalique situ pyramidum altius;*" "royal," *regius;* (2) "on high," *in altum;* (3) "repel," *defendo;* (4) "as it flies" (partic.)

VI. (1) "Distract," *torqueo;* "passionate," *aeger;* (2) "anything whatever," *quidvis;* (3) "for them destined to live," *victuris;* (4) "descendants," *postgeniti.*

EXERCISE XLIV

If thou wouldst find what holiest men have sought,
    Communion with the power of poesy,
Empty thy mind of all unquiet thought,
    Lay bare thy spirit to the vaulting sky
And glory of the sunshine; go and stand
    Where nodding briars sport with the water-break,
    Or by the plashings of a moonlit creek,
Or breast the wind upon some jutting land.
The most unheeded things have influences
    That sink into the soul: in after hours
We oft are tempted suddenly to dress
    The tombs of half-forgotten thought with flowers;
Our own choice mocks us, and the sweetest themes
Come to us without thought, like wayward dreams.

RETRANSLATION

I

If thy mind leads thee in a desire to follow (2) afar off the hard *footsteps* of holy men, (3, 4) and in thought to penetrate the mysterious sacred rites of the ninefold band,

II

banish far from thy bosom *the brood* of cares; (2) and thy heart (acc.) free from indulgences (3) open out beneath the bright rays of Phœbus (4) and the arched roof of the enchanting sky.

III

Go where briars *join* with the cascades in sportive (2) frolic, or (where) the winding (3) waters murmur in the moonlight; (4) or if it pleases (thee) on some cliff, to the storm

IV

to expose thy breast. In truth *from* the inmost (2) *heart* (our wish) brings forth secret things and not before recognised; (3) and with garlands the neglected (4) tomb of Memory to adorn

V

does a lively impulse constrain (us); and yet (2) our own purpose mocks us: whatever delightful (thought) (3) eluded (us), as at times of wayward (4) sleep the phantoms, comes back unsought.

HINTS

I. (1) "In a desire," *volentem:* comp. also Ov. *Met.* i. 1, "in nova fert animus," etc; (2) "hard," *difficilis;* "holy," *pius;* (3) "mysterious," *arcanus:* comp. Hor. *Od.* iii. 2. 27, "qui Cereris sacrum volgarit arcanae;" "ninefold," *novenus*.

II. (1) "Banish," *dispello;* (2) "brood," *examen;* (3) "bright rays," *nitores;* (4) "enchanting," *magicus*.

III. (1) "Join in" (line 2), *remisceo* (with acc.); "cascade," *scatebrae;* (3) "waters," *fluenta;* "murmur," *susurro*.

IV. (1) "From the inmost heart," *intimo* (line 1) *de corde* (line 3); (2) "our wish" (understood from *voluntas* in V. 1); (2) "and not before recognised," *nec prius agnita;* (4) "Memory," *Mnemosyne* (gen. -*es*).

V. (1) "Lively impulse," *voluntas vivida;* "and yet . . . us" (end the line with *nos tamen*); (2) "delightful (thought)," *amabile;* (3) "elude," *fallo;* (4) "phantoms," *simulacra;* "unsought," *sponte*.

EXERCISE XLV

When I survey the bright
    Cœlestiall spheare:
So rich with jewels hung that night
Doth like an Æthiop bride appeare,

My soul her wings doth spread
    And heaven-ward flies,
Th' Almighty's mysteries to read
In the large volumes of the skies.

For the bright firmament
    Shootes forth no flame
So silent, but is eloquent
In speaking the Creator's name.

No unregarded star
    Contracts its light
Into so small a character,
Remov'd far from our humane sight:

But if we stedfast looke,
    We shall discerne
In it, as in some holy booke,
How men may heavenly knowledge learne.

                        HABINGTON, *Castara.*

RETRANSLATION

I

When I behold the glittering firmament, (2) where the

brightness of spangled jewels (3) shines, and *the shades* of night, *like* an Eastern (4) bride, are lustrous;

II

the wing of my mind expands, and *away to* the pathless (2) heavens it flies; (3) *where*, through golden *courts* far and wide inscribed (acc.), (4) I survey the characters of God plain-to-read.

III

Whether farther from the depths there shines out (2) a glowing constellation, with no silent *brilliancy* in its course (3, 4) does it seem to celebrate the name of its Divine Artificer;

IV

or does it chance that a tinier star its flame (acc.) (2) contracts with dimmer torch, (3) not even does it with remote gleam (4) so faint (nom.) shun the sight,

V

but that the hearts of the gazers (*as if* a most sacred (2) page were laid open) (3, 4) learn to hear the heavenly messengers, and to know the very records of God.

Hints

I. (1) "When," *quando*; "glittering," *coruscus*; (2) "spangled," "variegated," *daedalus* (a favourite word with Lucr.); "jewels," lit. "jasper stones," *iaspides*: comp. Verg. Aen. iv. 261; (4) "like:" comp. "Lacaenae *more*," Hor. Od. ii. 11. 23; "bride," *nŭrus*, "are lustrous," *radiant*.

II. (1) "Expands," *sese . . . pandit*; (2) "away to," "right to," *ad usque*; "heavens" (the plural form *caelos* is found in Lucr. ii.

1097, but otherwise it wants classical authority); (3) "courts," *aulas;* "inscribed" (n. pl., to agree with *signa* in line 4); (4) "plain to read," *manifesta.*

III. (1) "The Depths," *profundum;* "shines out," *emicat;* (2) "glowing," *illustre;* "in its course," *vagum;* (3) "brilliancy," *fulgor.*

IV. (1) "Does it chance that," *forte;* "tiny," *minutus;* (2) "dim," *obscurus;* "torch," *lampăs, -ădis;* (3) "not (even) does it," *non illa;* "remote," *rēmotus;* (4) "faint," *tenuis;* "shun the sight:" comp. Hor. *Od.* i. 1. 34, " refugit tendere barbiton."

V. (1) "But that," *quin* (with subj.); "gazers," *obtuentes;* (2) "as if," *ceu* (with imp. subj.); (4) "learn" (last word in line 4), "records," *monimenta.*

EXERCISE XLVI

Moses seeing the Promised Land

My Father's hope! my childhood's dream!
    The promise from on high!
Long waited for! its glories beam
    Now when my death is nigh.

My death is come, but not decay;
    Nor eye nor mind is dim;
The keenness of youth's vigorous day
    Thrills in each nerve and limb.

Blest scene! thrice welcome after toil,
    If no deceit I view;
Oh might my lips but press the soil
    And prove the vision true!

Its glorious heights, its wealthy plains,
    Its many-tinted groves,

>   They call! but He my steps restrains
>   Who chastens whom He loves.
>
>   Ah! now they melt—they are but shades—
>   I die! yet is no rest,
>   O Lord, in store, since Canaan fades
>   But seen, and not possest?
>
> NEWMAN.

RETRANSLATION

I

Last care of (our) fathers, of *my* boyhood (2) first hope, from the high summit (3) sent-down the light of heaven hath shone, (4) too late, alas! as fate is approaching.

II

Me a too-swift death snatches-untimely in-my-vigour; (2) not dull is my mind, not dazed my eyes; (3) through my limbs and well-knit *frame* the glow (4) of youth thrills in due course.

III

Happy scene! now toils are done, (2) if thou showest what is true. O! that I on the ground (3) reclining might feel my imprinted (4) lips grow warm with the touch (of it) alone.

IV

How *bright* soever *thou art* with many-tinted woods (2) and with gold, yet (He) stays my footstep, (3) who knows-how with kindly (4) chastisements to restrain the reluctant mind.

V

Now I fade, and the beloved *land* melts away. (2) What rest, Father, dost thou promise, (3, 4) if the fields of a receding Canaan, once seen, withdraw themselves?

Hints

I. (1) "My" (line 2), *nostrae;* "boyhood," *puerītia* (syncopated, as in Hor. *Od.* i. 26. 8, "actae non alio rege puertiae"); (2) "high," *arduus;* (4) "as fate is" (abl. abs.).

II. (1) "Untimely," expressed by prefix *prae-;* "in my vigour," *vigens;* (2) "is dull," *hebescit* (turn "are dazed" similarly, by using *stupeo*); (3) "well-knit," *conexus;* (4) "of youth" (adj.); "thrills," *salit;* "in due course," *rite.*

III. (1) "Scene:" there is no word in Latin for "scenery" or "a picturesque scene," but Virgil uses *scaena* (*Aen.* i. 164) for the background of a view, "tum silvis scaena coruscis," and that word may serve here; (3) "my imprinted," *defixa;* (4) "to grow warm" (of an instantaneous act), pf. inf.; "alone," *merus.*

IV. (1) "How . . . soever," *utcumque;* "many-tinted," *versicolor;* (2) "thou art bright," *luces;* (3) "kindly," *benignus;* (4) "chastisements," *supplicia;* "reluctant" (to come in line 3).

V. (1) "I fade," lit. "am being dissolved," *solvor* (use the same verb, reflexively, for "melts away);" "beloved," *amabilis;* (2) "promise," *adnuo;* (3) "receding," *fugiens* (in line 4); "Canaan," *Palaestina;* "withdraw themselves," sc . . . *recepto* (line 3).

EXERCISE XLVII

My heart is disquieted within me,
And the fear of death is fallen upon me.
Fearfulness and trembling are come upon me,
And an horrible dread hath overwhelmed me.

And I said, O that I had wings like a dove,
For then would I flee away and be at rest.
Lo, then would I get me away far off,
And remain in the wilderness.
I would make haste to escape,
Because of the stormy wind and tempest.

PSALM lv. 4-7.

RETRANSLATION

I

My heart is throbbing with restless waves, (2) agitated with fear foreboding death. (3) In my dread of what is to come, trembling (4) has convulsed my lifeless limbs.

II

O that I could glide with a winged dove's (2) flight! I said: Soon would I hide myself, (3) where on distant shores (4) it may be allowed a secluded one to enjoy peace.

III

So great a love of flight (is there) *to one longing for* sequestered lands; (2) in his anxiety, that is, (3) to shun the beating tempest's (4) blasts, and the north-wind's heavy wrath.

HINTS

I. (1) "Is throbbing," *aestuat*; (2) "agitated:" comp. Pers. ii. 54, "lactari praetrepidum cor;" "foreboding," *ominatus*; (3) "in my dread of" (use genit. of partic., with *mei* understood, depending on *artus*).

II. "O that" (*o ut* or *o si?*); (2) "flight," *volatus*; "would I hide myself," *conderer*; (3) "where:" comp. Hor. *Od.* iii. 3. 55, "*qua parte* debacchentur ignes;" (4) "a secluded one," *repostus*.

III. (1) "sequestered lands," *amota terrae ;* (2) "to one longing for" (with the idea of not being able to obtain), *desideranti ;* "in his anxiety" (dat. of adj.) ; "that is," *scilicet ;* (3) "beating," comp. Lucr. vi. 115, "verberibus venti versant *plangun*tque."

EXERCISE XLVIII[1]

Whom we see not we revere ;
We revere, and we refrain
From talk of battles loud and vain,
And brawling memories all too free
For such a wise humility
As befits a solemn fane :
We revere, and while we hear
The tides of Music's golden sea
Setting toward eternity,
Uplifted high in heart and hope are we,
Until we doubt not that for one so true
There must be other nobler work to do
Than when he fought at Waterloo,
And victor he must ever be.
For though the Giant Ages heave the hill
And break the shore, and evermore
Make and break, and work their will ;
Tho' world on world in myriad myriads roll
Around us, each with different powers,
And other forms of life than ours,
What know we greater than the soul ?
On God and Godlike men we build our trust.

TENNYSON.

[1] This and the next Exercise are in First Asclepiad metre. See the Introduction, p. xxxvii.

RETRANSLATION

I

Revering an absent one *a nation* keeps silence, nor (2) for noise of battles, (mere) empty rumours, (3) now cares; nor (cares) reckless (4) stories to hear, *words* full of license

II

and all unworthy of a religious silence. (2) An absent one we respect: there-is-eddying a golden (3) minstrelsy of harps on the heavenly way: (4) so do we also uplift our hopes, our heart

III

on high to the powers above; doubtless a higher (2) life yonder awaits so great a soul; there awaits (3) the conqueror a laurel better than the Belgian, (4) surviving (acc.), I trow, when death is overcome.

IV

For though the great ages upheave the mountains, (2) (and) shake the dry-land; (and though) *nature* remake what is made, (3) and be ever playing the part of a mistress; (4) (though) the stars in varying office on their everlasting

V

course roll in countless numbers, (2) and develope their own forms of life, (3) yet still the force of fiery intellect sways all things alike; (4) we trust in divine souls and in God.

Hints

I. (1) "A nation," *populus*, to come in line 3; "keeps (a religious) silence:" comp. Verg. Aen. v. 71, "ore favete omnes;" Hor. *Od.* iii. 1. 2, "favete linguis;" (2) "for" (sign of acc.).

II. (1) "And all," *atque*; (2) "there is eddying," *fluctuat*; "so," *sic*, to be repeated with *animum*.

III. (1) "To the powers above," *superis*; (4) "surviving" acc. to agree with *victorem*); "I trow," *credo*.

IV. (1) "For though," *etenim*, with subj.; (2) "dry land," *terrenum*; "remake," *reficio* (pf. subj.); (3) "the part," *vices*; (4) "on" (sign of acc.).

V. (1) "Course," *viam*; (2) "forms," *facies*; (3) "all things alike," *cuncta*.

EXERCISE XLIX

Loving she is, and tractable, though wild:
And innocence hath privilege in her
To dignify arch looks, and laughing eyes,
And feats of cunning, and the pretty round
Of trespasses, affected to provoke
Mock chastisement and partnership in play.
And as a faggot sparkles on the hearth
Not less if unattended and alone,
Than when both young and old sit gather'd round
And take delight in its activity,
Even so this happy creature of herself
Is all-sufficient; solitude to her
Is blithe society, who fills the air
With gladness and involuntary songs.
Light are her sallies as the tripping fawn's
Forth startled from the fern where she lay couch'd.

*   *   *   *

WORDSWORTH.

RETRANSLATION

I

Gentle she is, and teachable, though she be wild, (2) and (one) whom *in her innocence* a pleasing archness of the eye (3) and mischievous look misbecomes not; (4) nor ensnaring wiles, nor in alternate change

II

loveable sport, mimicking a fault, (2) soon to delight in being punished. (3) As a brand on the hearth sparkles no less, (4) shining all by itself, than if youths together

III

and old men close-gathered were sitting by (2) to watch the living flame play; (3) so too the little girl of-three-years for herself alone (4) both sufficed, enjoying her own gladness,

IV

and in lonely places there is a welcome *throng* of companions, (2) singing together in the empty air. (3) Then too she often flies, as with free footstep (4) the fawn bounds forth from the close covert.

Hints

I. (1) "Gentle," "winning," *blandus*; "though," *licet* (with subj.); "wild," comp. of *acer*; "in her innocence" (adj.), *innocuus* (line 3); "archness," *protervitas*; (4) "nor" (continue with *que*); "in alternate change," *vice mutua*.

II. (1) "Mimicking," *simulans*; "fault," *peccatum*; (2) "soon to delight in," *quod mox* with subj. (one of the uses called "consecutive"); "being punished" (pres. inf. pass.), use the phrase *supplicio adficere*;

(3) "brand," *taeda*; (4) "all by itself," *secum solā*; "if" (to come in next line).

III. (1) "Close-gathered," *conferti*; (2) "to watch" (*qui* with "final" subj., to be distinguished from the use in II. 2); "flame," *flammula* (to avoid the diminutive, *flammam* . . . *mobilem* may be used instead); "of three years old," *trima*; (4) "both sufficed," *suffecitque*.

IV. (1) "There is," *est* (to come in line 2): comp. also Tibull. iv. 13. 12, "in solis tu mihi turba locis;" (2) "singing together" (relat. with subj. of *concino*, as in II. 2); (3) "often," *crebra* (adj. with adverbial force; see Introd., p. xlviii); (4) "covert," lit. "brambles," *vepres*.

EXERCISE L[1]

When Nature tries her finest touch,
    Weaving her vernal wreath,
Mark ye how close she veils her round,
Not to be traced by sight or sound,
    Nor soil'd by ruder breath.

Who ever saw the earliest rose
    First open her sweet breast?
Or, when the summer sun goes down,
The first soft star in evening's crown
    Light up her gleaming crest?

But there's a sweeter flower than e'er
    Blush'd on the rosy spray—
A brighter star, a richer bloom,
Than e'er did western heaven illume
    At close of summer day.

---

[1] This and the next two Exercises are in Second Asclepiad metre. See the Introduction, p. xxxvii.

'Tis Love, the last, best gift of heaven;
    Love gentle, holy, pure;
But, tenderer than a dove's soft eye,
The searching sun, the open sky,
    She never could endure.
KEBLE.

RETRANSLATION

I

When nature, wishing to be fairer to the sight, (2) weaves a lovely garland in fresh spring, (3) she retires for a little into herself, that uncongenial (4) winds may not dash away the flower;

II

and, shrinking-from the gaze, covers *close* with a veil (2) her sweet cheeks. When did *the first* rose (3) to the searching eyes of men its perfumed (4) bosom unfold at birth?

III

Who has beheld when, as the sun goes down, (2) a star shining at eve with glittering crest (3) first comes forth from the sky? (3, 4) But yet there is a flower better than the flower of the crimson rose,

IV

whatever (rose) gleams on the spreading tree; (2) there is a star, with which in lovely radiance strives (3) in vain the star in its tender blush, (3, 4) whatever (star) twinkles through the western heavens.

v

In truth it is gentle love, the latest gift (pl.) (2) of heaven, pure love, and (love) which in its tenderness (3) vanquishing in softness the golden eyes of the turtle-dove, (4) could not endure the sun.

Hints

I. (1) "To the sight," *adspici.* For the inf. comp. Hor. *Od.* i. 19. 8, "et voltus nimium lubricus adspici;" (3) "retires," *redit;* "uncongenial," *male dispares:* for the force of *male*, see Introd., p. xlix; (4) "winds," *noti;* see Introd., p. xlviii.

II. (1) "Shrink-from," *tremo* (with acc.); "veil," prop. "bridal veil" (dim.), *flammeolum;* (2) *close*, fem. adj.; (3) "searching," *petens;* "of men" (to come in line 2); (4) "at birth," *nascens.*

III. (1) "Who has beheld when," lit. "who beholding (abl. abs.), does," etc.; (2) "crest," *comae* (to come in line 1); "at eve" (adj.), *vespertinus;* (3) "sky," *polus;* (4) "better than," *prior* (with abl.); "crimson," *puniceus.*

IV. (1) "Whatever," *quaecumque* (with subj.); but for the restraining arrangement of the lines, this would be translated "better than the flower of any rose that gleams," etc.; "spreading:" comp. Verg. *Aen.* i. 1; (2) "with which" (dat.); "radiance," *radius;* (3) "in its tender blush," *molle rubens;* "heavens," *aether.*

V. (1) "In truth," *nempe;* "latest," *novissimus,* (2) "in its tenderness" (nom. adj.); (3) "eyes" (to come in line 2); (4) "could not," *non potuit.*

EXERCISE LI

O bliss, when, all in circle drawn
    About him, heart and ear were fed
    To hear him, as he lay and read
The Tuscan poets on the lawn:

Or in the all-golden afternoon
   A guest, or happy sister, sung,
   Or here she brought the harp, and flung
A ballad to the brightening moon.

Nor less it pleased in livelier moods
   Beyond the bounding hill to stray,
   And break the livelong summer day
With banquet in the distant woods;

Whereat we glanced from theme to theme,
   Discuss'd the books to love or hate,
   Or touch'd the changes of the state,
Or threaded some Socratic dream.
                              TENNYSON.

RETRANSLATION

I

Happy (we), as often as a group of companions, (2) all hanging on thee, delighted to feed (3) (their) ears, while lying under a plane-tree the numbers (acc.) (4) of the Tuscan fathers thou wouldst read.

II

Or if a guest at leisure, or it might be, as the golden (2) noon declined, a glad sister, (3) carelessly striking the harp, *sings of* the growing (4) brightness of the moon.

III

But if it rather pleased (us) at festive time (2) to bend

our course beyond the verge of the mountains, and (3) reclining far away in a summery vale (4) to take a portion from the day,

IV

(then) we delighted to glance at the affairs and books of men, (2) to which one praise was due, to which censure; (3) and the changes of state, and the Socratic school's (4) secret intricacies (we delighted) to inquire into.

Hints

I. (1) "Companions," *sodales;* (2) "all hanging," *tota inhians.*

II. (1) "Or it might be," *seu libet;* (3) "carelessly:" comp. Hor. *Od.* ii. 11. 14, "iacentes sic temere;" "strike," *increpo* (with abl.): comp. Verg. *Aen.* xii. 332, "Sanguineus Mavors clupeo increpat;" in Hor. *Od.* iv. 15. 2, "increpuit lyra," there is the idea of chiding; (4) "sings of," *concelabrat.*

III. (2) "Verge," *limen;* (3) "reclining," *cubantibus,* dat. after *placuit* above; "to take," etc.: comp. Hor. *Od.* i. 1. 20, "partem solido demere de die."

IV. (1) "Glance at," "touch upon," *tangere;* (2) "to which one," *cuinam;* (3) "of state" (adj.); "school:" comp. Hor. *Od.* i. 29. 14, "Socraticam et domum;" (4) "intricacies," *ambages.*

EXERCISE LII

A Baby's Epitaph

April made me: winter laid me here away asleep.
Bright as Maytime was my daytime; night is soft and deep:
Though the morrow bring forth sorrow, well are ye that
    weep.

Ye that held me dear beheld me not a twelvemonth long:
All the while ye saw me smile, ye knew not whence the song
Came that made me smile, and laid me here, and wrought
  you wrong.

Angels, calling from your brawling world one undefiled,
Homeward bade me, and forbade me here to rest beguiled:
Here I sleep not: pass, and weep not here upon your child.
                                A. C. SWINBURNE.

RETRANSLATION

I

April brought (me) forth; winter laid (me) here (2) asleep in the grave: brighter than spring (3) shone my life: now kindly *night* closes my eyes, (4) and for *you* mourners a sad

II

morn arises, yet not without God's providence. (2) In truth, for scarce a whole year was I among (3) the bosoms of dear ones; at which time (4) you might have marked (my) light laugh:

III

But the fount of (my) joy conceals its sources, (2) and (so does) the divine melody; the which when once with my ears (3) I caught, ye seek (me) grudgingly laid here to rest. (4) But indeed a heavenly *messenger*, homeward

IV

summoning me from the din of earth, (2) forbade a pure soul to be ensnared with empty hope. (3) Not here (is) my rest: *your child* bids you take (4) your way with tearless eyes.

Hints

I. (1) "Bring forth," *gigno;* "lay," *condo;* (2) "bright," *nitens;* (3) "close," *comprimo;* (4) "mourners" (partic.).

II. (1) "Without God's providence:" comp. Hor. *Od.* iii. 4. 20, "*non sine dis animosus infans;*" (2) "in truth," *scilicet;* "to be among," *interesse* (with dat.); (4) "you might," *fas erat;* "light" (to come in preceding line).

III. (1) "Conceals," etc. : comp. Hor. *Od.* iv. 14. 45, "fontium qui celat origines;" (2) "once" (*quondam* or *semel?*); (3) "I caught" (use the abl. absol.); "grudgingly:" comp. Hor. *Od.* iii. 24. 32, "sublatam ex oculis quaerimus invidi;" "laid to rest," *positum;* (4) "but indeed," *sed enim.*

IV. (1) "Of earth" (adj.); (2) "to be ensnared," *capi;* (3, 4), "your child," *nata;* "take your way," *carpere . . . viam;* "with tearless eyes:" comp. Hor. *Od.* i. 3. 18, "qui siccis oculis . . . vidit."

EXERCISE LIII[1]

Sonnet, 1857

My youth is passing from me: in life's May
    My deeds, poor fool! are dreams and reverie,
Changeful as clouds upon a summer day,
    That touch not earth. And all things chide me; yea,
        As I o'erleaped a rivulet, ceaselessly
        With all its mountain-music rushing by,
The glad stream and its ever-onward flow
Made my heart gush with sorrow, that but I

---

[1] Exercises LIII.-LVI. are in Third Asclepiad metre. See the Introduction, p. xxxviii.

Stand idle, and am making for no shore.
Sweet monitor! but, long ere winter hoar,
I will be pressing on to Helicon,
My glorious goal; and if I can no more,
Like thee, I'll nurse some floweret of my own,
To glad young hearts, and bloom, when I am gone.

J. H. BURROW.[1]

RETRANSLATION

I

My years are passing by: (2) in life's fresh flower on naught save *light* dreams (3) intent do I waste time, (4) infatuated one! But they meanwhile change their forms,

II

as on a summer day (2) a cloud spurns the earth in airy flight. (3) Whatever I see chides me (4) as a loiterer. Lo! where *a rivulet* hurrying rolls its waters,

III

not without echo of mountain, (2) sweetly prattling, bent on following its course. (3) It (acc.) by chance with roaming footstep (4) I lately leapt across: but with sudden *tears* my

IV

cheeks were bedewed, (2) as I grieved that thus far I was not seeking of my way (3) a goal, alone idle, as (4) the rivulet that admonishes me with its waters. But ere

[1] B.A., St. Cath. Coll., Cambridge, 1855, *ob.* June 20, 1876. "His saltem accumulem donis."

V

that the hoary snows return, (2) I will steadfastly direct my course, whither glory calls (me) (3) and the abodes of Helicon. (4) And if I avail not aught besides, after thy

VI

pattern, fleeting stream, I will nourish (2) a flower, such as children with *merry* hand (3) may delight to gather, (4) living (acc.) after the death of the hapless poet.

Hints

I. (2) "On nought save," *nil nisi*; (3) "waste time," *mŏror*.

II. (1) "But they," *quae*; "change their forms:" comp. Verg. Aen. ix. 164, "discurrunt variantque vices;" (2) "spurns:" comp. Hor. Od. iii. 2. 24, "spernit humum fugiente penna;" (3) "chide," *increpo*; (4) "as a loiterer," *cessantem*; "rivulet" (to come in III. 2); "rolls," *agit*.

III. (1) "Echo," *murmur*; (2) "prattling," *loquax*; "bent on," *certus* (with inf.).

IV. (1) "Were bedewed," *suffusae (sunt)*; (2) "as I grieved" (dat. of partic.); "thus far," *adhuc*; (3) "idle," *iners*; (4) "ere," *prius*, followed by *quam* beginning the next line.

V. (2) "Steadfastly," *certus*; (3) "of Helicon" (adj.), *Hĕlĭcōnius*; (4) "after" (sign of abl.)

VI. (1) "Pattern," *ritus*: comp. Hor. Od. iii. 14. 1, "Herculis ritu;" (2) "stream," *lympha*; "such as," *si quis erit quem*; (3) "may delight," use the impers. constr. with *juvet*; "to gather:" comp. Hor. Od. i. 1. 4; (4) "living," *vividus*; "death," *funus* (pl.)

EXERCISES LIV, LV

The world's great age begins anew,
The golden years return,

The earth doth like a snake renew
    Her winter weeds outworn.

A brighter Hellas rears its mountains
    From waves serener far;
A new Peneus rolls its fountains
    Against the morning star.
Where fairer Tempes bloom, there sleep
Young Cyclads on a sunnier deep.

A loftier Argo cleaves the main,
    Fraught with a later prize;
Another Orpheus sings again,
    And loves, and weeps, and dies.
A new Ulysses leaves once more
Calypso for his native shore.

O write no more the tale of Troy,
    If earth Death's scroll must be!
Nor mix with Laian rage the joy
    Which dawns upon the free:
Although a subtler Sphinx renew
Riddles of death Thebes never knew.

Another Athens shall arise,
    And to remoter time
Bequeath, like sunset to the skies,
    The splendour of its prime,
And leave, if nought so bright may live,
All earth can take, or heaven can give.
                      SHELLEY.

RETRANSLATION

I

Anew has the great order (2) of the centuries come round; there is born a golden (3) age; her weeds, by the buffetings (4) of winter worn out, does the earth, like a serpent, renew.

II

Now at length a brighter *Hellas* rears (2) (its) mountains from clearer waters: (3) against the morning star does a new (4) Peneus roll (its) lovely tides.

III

A fairer Tempe blooms, (2) and Cȳclădĕs lie slumbering on the deep, (3) where laughs a brighter sun. (4) Lo! a nobler Argō cleaves the open sea,

IV

which bears other merchandise; (2) another Orpheus loves, weeps, sings, and perishes. (3) *Laertes' son* visits the shores of his fatherland, (4) which he has preferred to a goddess.

V

Write not the tale of Troy (2) if the title of Death is to be written on the earth; (3) or mix with the frenzies (4) of Laius the joys that have been given to the free,

VI

though more deadly *wiles* (acc.) a Sphinx (2) subtler than the Theban renew. (3) Other sons of Athens shall arise, (4) and to remotest time a ray (acc.) of splendour, like the setting sun to the sky, (2) shall diffuse, and *shall leave behind* all the blessings that earth can enjoy, (3) all that heaven (can) give, (4) if things that are too bright may not live.

HINTS

I. (1) "Anew:" comp. Verg. *Ecl.* iv. 5, "Magnus *ab intĕgro* saeclorum nascitur ordo," which will suggest other words also; (2) "come round," *redeo*; (3) "weeds," lit. "slough," *exuviae*; "buffetings," lit. "threats;" (4) "serpent," *coluber*.

II. (3) "Morning star," *Lucifer*; (4) "Peneus:" comp. Ov. *Met.* i. 569, "vocant Tempe, per quae Pēnēŭs, ab imo | effusus Pindo," etc. Hence Shelley's line, "Liquid Pĕneus was | flowing," is wrongly scanned "Liquid | Peneus was | flowing" in Latham's *English Language* (p. 520); "tides," *latices*.

III. (1) "Fairer," use *magis*; "Tempe," Greek neut. pl.: comp. Hor. *Od.* i. 7. 4, "Thessala Tempē," and above, on II. 4; (2) "slumbering," *sopitae*; (4) "open sea," *pelagus*: comp. Verg. *Aen.* v. 8.

IV. (1) "Other," "another" (of two), *alter*; (3) "Laertes' son" (in line 4), *Laërtiades*; (4) "has preferred to:" note that, besides the construction like the English, as in "Judex honestum praetulit utile" (*Od.* iv. 9. 41), a converse one may be used, with *posthabere* or *postponere*.

V. (1) "Write not," *noli*, etc., and comp. Juv. *Sat.* viii. 221, "*Troica* non scripsit;" (2) "Death," *nex*; "is to be written," fut. pft.; (3) "mix," inf. depending on *noli*; (4) "of Laius" (dissyll.).

VI. (1) "Though," *ut*: comp. Ov. *Ep. ex P.* iii. 4. 79, "Ut desint vires, tamen est laudanda voluntas;" "more," *magis*; (3) "sons of Athens," *Cecropidae*; (4) "ray," *facem*.

VII. (2) All . . . that," *quot*; (2) "leave behind" (in line 3), *desero*; (4) "things that are too bright," *quae fulgent nimium*; "may not," *nefas*, with inf.

EXERCISE LVI

Avenge, O Lord, thy slaughter'd saints, whose bones
Lie scatter'd on the Alpine mountains cold;

> Ev'n them who kept thy truth so pure of old,
> When all our fathers worshipt stocks and stones,
> Forget not: in thy book record their groans
>   Who were thy sheep, and in their ancient fold
>   Slain by the bloody Piedmontese, that roll'd
> Mother with infant down the rocks. Their moans
>   The vales redoubled to the hills, and they
> To heav'n. Their martyr'd blood and ashes sow
>   O'er all th' Italian fields, where still doth sway
> The triple Tyrant; that from these may grow
>   A hundred-fold, who having learn'd thy way
> Early may fly the Babylonian woe.
>
> MILTON.

RETRANSLATION

I

Be present, Almighty One, to thine own, (2) whose bones lie scattered over Alpine (3) snows; to whom thy truth (4) (was) hallowed of old, while (our) fathers, an ignorant race,

II

worshipped (pres.) both stocks and stones. (2, 3) O! be present, and from (thy) recording mind let there not fall the cries of thy flock, (4) which (acc.) in its native folds there massacres,

III

alas! the savage race of Italians, (2) and hurls-headlong from the cliffs mothers and children: (3) but the valley (redoubles) to the heights (4) (their) wailings, and the mountain redoubles (them) to thy heaven.

IV

Let (their) *blood* live on the Italian plain (2) prolific, and (their) ashes scattered o'er the land, (3) where still the dread king on the *triple* height (4) is-cruel: so for thee a manifold

V

offspring shall arise, in thy (2) law trained; which (offspring) the Babylonian woe (3) and the guile of the old way (4) may wisely shun with early step.

Hints

I. (2, 3) "Alpine snows," *Alpium frigus;* (3) "truth," *veritas.*
II. (2, 3) "Cries," *voces* (in line 3); "recording," *memori* (in line 2); (4) "massacres," *foede necat.*
III. (3) "Valley," *convallis;* (4) "heaven," *polus.*
IV. (1) "Prolific," *fecundus;* (3) "triple," *tergeminus.*
V. (2) "In thy law trained," *tuum fas edocta;* (4) "shun," *effugio.*

EXERCISE LVII[1]

Though the torrents from their fountains
    Roar down many a craggy steep,
Yet they find among the mountains
    Resting-places calm and deep.

Clouds that love through air to hasten,
    Ere the storm its fury stills,
Helmet-like themselves will fasten
    On the heads of towering hills.

---

[1] Exercises LVII.-LXV. are in Fourth Asclepiad metre. See the Introduction, p. xxxviii.

If on windy days the raven
　　Gambol like a dancing skiff,
None the less she loves her haven
　　In the bosom of the cliff.

Day and night my toils redouble,
　　Never nearer to the goal;
Night and day I feel the trouble
　　Of the wanderer in my soul.

　　　　　　　　　　WORDSWORTH.

RETRANSLATION

I

Though with hoarse-sounding *roar*, issuing from their fountains, (2) the torrents chafe against the crags, (3) still in peace beneath the lofty (4) mountain they may rest.

II

Clouds, which a rougher breeze is chasing, (2) as often as the fury of the storms is hushed (3) *hang* motionless over the lofty (4) hills, like helmets.

III

Nay, if the raven, like a winged skiff, (2) scuds hither and thither, when the wind is fresher, (3) still *it loves* to glide down and hide itself (4) at last in the bosom of the cliff.

IV

But the sun and the returning night (only) double for me (2) my cares: the goal recedes while it is pursued: (3) in truth I am tormented *with a thirst* for wandering (4) night and day.

HINTS

I. (1) "Hoarse-sounding," *raucisonus;* "issuing," *exeltus;* (2) "chafe against:" comp. Hor. *Od.* iv. 14. 48, "obstrepit Oceanus Britannis;" (3) "in peace," *tranquillus* (dat.); (4) "they may," *fas* (sc. *eis est*).

II. (1) "Rougher," *violentior;* (2) "storms," *nimbi;* (4) "hills," *iuga;* "like helmets," *ecu galeae.*

III. (1) "Nay," *quin;* "winged," *volatilis;* (2) "scuds," *rapitur;* "fresher," *acrior;* (3) "to glide . . . and" (use partic.); "hide itself," *abdi* (pass. form in middle sense).

IV. (1) "Double," *duplico* (sing.); (2) "recedes," *fugit retro:* comp. Verg. *Aen.* iii. 496; "pursue," *peto;* (3) "in truth," *quippe;* "for wandering" (genit. of gerund); (4) "night and day," *noctes perque dies.*

EXERCISE LVIII

Fair ship, that from the Italian shore
    Sailest the placid ocean-plains
    With my lost Arthur's loved remains,
Spread thy full wings and waft him o'er.

So draw him home to those that mourn
    In vain; a favourable speed
    Ruffle thy mirror'd mast, and lead
Thro' prosperous floods his holy urn.

All night no ruder air perplex
    Thy sliding keel, till Phosphor, bright
    As our pure love, thro' early light
Shall glimmer on the dewy decks.

Sphere all your lights around, above;
    Sleep, gentle heav'ns, before the prow;
    Sleep, gentle winds, as he sleeps now,
My friend, the brother of my love,

My Arthur, whom I shall not see
   Till all my widow'd race be run;
   Dear as the mother to the son,
More than my brothers are to me.

TENNYSON.

RETRANSLATION

I

O *ship*, that sailest through the calm sea, (2) putting off from Italian shores, (3) and bringest back *my* Arthur's (4) dear remains;

II

spread (thy) full sails, and over the waters (2) borne hither restore (him) to his companions sorrowing, (3) alas! in vain. For thee (4) may a prosperous course *ruffle* the image of thy mast

III

on the surface of the waters, and through favouring (2) floods may it duly waft-on (his) sacred urn. (3) To thy keel all night (4) nowhere may a too boisterous

IV

wind be adverse, as it glides; *till* on the dewy (2) deck at early morn thou shinest, (3) Phosphorus, shedding a pure (4) ray, like our love.

V

In the vaulted sky let all the stars hang (motionless); (2) let *slumber* hold you, O clouds, (and) you too, O winds, (3) such as now holds him, (4) a part (acc.) of our soul.

VI

O Arthur, denied, alas! to my eyes, (2) till I shall have finished my widowed course; (3) not equal to thee (are) brothers to me, (4) nor a mother to her own son.

Hints

I. (1) "Sail," *velifico*; (2) "put off from," *solvo* (with abl.); (3) "Arthur," *Arturus*.

II. (1) "Sails," *sinus*; "waters," *aequora*; (2) "borne hither," *advectus*; (3) "mast," *malus* (to come at the end of this line).

III. (1) "Ruffle," *frango*; (2) "floods," *aequora*; "waft-on," *proveho*; (3) "all night" (abl.); (4) "boisterous," *violens*.

IV. (1) "Be adverse," *obficere*; "dewy," *umidus*; (2) "deck," *puppis*; "shinest," *refulgeo* (fut. perf.)

V. (1) "Vaulted," *cavus*; (2) "slumber," *sopor* (to come at end of line 4); "winds," *flamina*; (4) comp. Hor. *Od.* i. 3. 8, "et serves animae dimidium meae."

VI. (2) "Till," *dum* (with fut. pft.); "equal to," *instar* (with gen.); "thee" (at end of line 2); (4) "mother," *genetrix*.

EXERCISE LIX

A Canticle to Apollo

Play, Phœbus, on thy lute,
And we will sit all mute,
By listening to thy lyre
That sets all ears on fire.

Hark, hark! the god does play;
And, as he leads the way
Through heaven, the very spheres
As men, turn all to ears.

HERRICK.

Retranslation

I

Phœbus, with (thy) right hand touch thy lyre, I pray; (2) we, the crowd of men, will sit mute; (3) 'twill be a delight to listen; (4) (our) ears burn with a strange fire.

II

Hark! the god has now touched the strings of his lute; (2) while he flies (as) a leader through the starry heaven, (3, 4) and the very zones in listening rival listening men.

Hints

I. (3) "To listen," *auscultare*; (4) "burn," *calent*.

II. (1) "Hark," *audin* (= *audisne*); (3, 4) "zones," *plāgae* (line 4); "in listening," etc., lit. "in ears rival (*aequant*, with acc.) men with ears" (*auritos*): comp. Hor. *Od.* i. 12. 11, "auritas . . . quercus."

EXERCISES LX, LXI

No war, or battle's sound
Was heard the world around:
   The idle spear and shield were high up hung,
The hooked chariot stood
Unstain'd with hostile blood,
   The trumpet spake not to the armed throng;
And kings sat still with awful eye,
As if they surely knew their sovran Lord was by.

But peaceful was the night,
Wherein the Prince of light
   His reign of peace upon the world began;

The winds, with wonder whist,
Smoothly the waters kist,
    Whisp'ring new joys to the mild ocean,
Who now hath quite forgot to rave,
While birds of calm sit brooding on the charmed wave.

The stars with deep amaze
Stand fix'd in stedfast gaze,
    Bending one way their precious influence,
And will not take their flight,
For all the morning light,
    Or Lucifer that often warn'd them thence.
MILTON.

RETRANSLATION

I

The uncertain roar of wars is hushed, (2) the brayings of the trumpet sound not in all the world; (3) now the spear is hung up (4) in the halls, and the heavy shield;

II

and the heavy, scythed chariots are silent, (2) unstained by the marks of an enemy's blood. (3) Now, well-nigh speechless, kings (4) with fixed eyes are silent,

III

conscious that they discern the Lord of kings. (2) But quiet repose brooded over the sky, (3) *when* the Prince, the source of light, (4) set foot upon the earth.

IV

In deep silence was that night passed, (2) inaugurating for the nations a peaceful reign, (3) when in-wonder there was laid, (4) the surface (acc.) of the *waves* of the rough sea

V

sweetly kissing, the breath of the south-wind; (2) and now to ocean fresh joys (acc.) gently (3) with mild voice whispering. (4) It (the ocean) is now silent, with settled

VI

waters pausing, while brooding lightly (2) on the calm sea the halcyon builds. (3) Fixed in silent gaze (4) the stars stand wondering,

VII

and with steadfast-regard bend low over their (2) King; nor does coming Lucifer chase (them) away, or (3) the morning *light* of day, (4) warning them to depart.

Hints

I. (1) "Is hushed," *conticesco* (pft.)

II. (1) "The heavy, scythed chariots" (turn by "the loads of the bent (*curvorum*) chariots"); (2) "an enemy's," *hosticus*.

III. (2) "Brooded," *incubo* (pft.); (3) "source," *auctor*.

IV. (2) "Inaugurating," *auspicans*; (3) "in wonder," *mirata*; (4) "the surface of," *summas*, to agree with the word for "waves" in V. 1.

V. (1) "Breath," *aura*, coming as the subject of "was laid" in the previous stanza; (3) "whispering," to agree with "breath" above; (4) "it," *qui*.

VI. (1) "Pausing," *intermissus*; (2) "the halcyon," *alcedo*.

VII. (1) "Steadfast regard," *obtutus*; "bend low over," *cominus inminent*; (3) "morning," adj.; (4) "warning," *praemonens*.

EXERCISES LXII, LXIII

King of kings and Lord of lords,
    Thus we move, our footsteps timing
    To our cymbals' faintest chiming,
Where Thy house its rest accords.

Chased and wounded birds are we,
Through the dark air fled to Thee;
To the shadow of Thy wings,
Lord of lords and King of kings.

Behold, O Lord, the heathen tread
    The branches of Thy fruitful vine,
Which its luxuriant tendrils spread
    O'er all the hills of Palestine.

And now the wild boar comes to waste
E'en us, the greenest boughs and last,
That, drinking of Thy choicest dew,
On Zion's hill in beauty grew.
                      MILMAN.

RETRANSLATION

I

O Almighty King, O God most good, (2) Thy temple (acc.), holy Father, we approach: (3) lo! how, a sorrowful band, (4) we drag our wearied footsteps,

II

and hardly do our cymbals chime in measure. (2) Thy temple, holy Father, we approach; (3) to sorrowful maidens will it (4) give peace and repose.

III

To Thee, as birds sore wounded, (2) through the gloomy darkness of the air are we come; (3, 4) let the protection of Thy wing extend its benign shade.

IV

Look back, mighty Father, on Thy vine; (2) the *profane enemy* hath defiled its bright tendrils in the dust; its sacred shoots beneath his feet (4) doth he trample,

V

which but lately, with the luxuriance of its tender foliage, (2) clothed the well-watered hills of the Israelites. (3) Upon us, upon us is rushing (4) now the wild-boar, (as) his last prey;

VI

whom ever green, ever lovely, (2) Sion saw stretching out glad branches, (3) and laughing, as we drank (4) the delights of Thy dew.

HINTS

I. (2) "Approach," *adgredior*; (3) "band," *caterva*; (4) "footstep," *pes*.

II. (1) "Chime," *concino*; "in measure," *in numerum*.

III. (1) "Sore wounded," *vulnere saucius*; (2) "air" (the lower), *aer*; (3) "benign," *mitis*.

IV. (1) "Look back on," *respicio*; see note on Ex. XXII. II. (3);
(2) "the profane enemy," *hostis* . . . *inpius* (to come in line 4);
(3) "shoots," *fetus* (sing.); (4) "trample," *protero*.

V. (1) "Which," *qui*, referring to *fetus*; "foliage," *coma*; (2) "well-watered," "moist," *uvidus*; "Israelites," *Isacidae*.

VI. (1) "Whom" (acc. pl. fem.) referring to *nos*; (2) "stretching" (pres. inf.); (3) "as we drank," *bibentes*.

EXERCISES LXIV, LXV

Lead, kindly light, amid the encircling gloom,
    Lead Thou me on:
The night is dark, and I am far from home,
    Lead thou me on:
Keep thou my feet; I do not ask to see
The distant scene; one step enough for me.

I was not ever thus, nor prayed that Thou
    Should'st lead me on:
I loved to choose and see my path, but now
    Lead Thou me on.
I loved the garish day, and, spite of fears,
Pride ruled my will: remember not past years.

So long Thy power hath blest me, sure it still
    Will lead me on
O'er moor and fen, o'er crag and torrent, till
    The night is gone,
And with the morn those angel faces smile,
Which I have loved long since, and lost awhile.

                              NEWMAN.

RETRANSLATION

I

O kindly light, onwards with good omen (2) lead for me, lead my steps bewildered in the gloom; (3) (for me) whom wandering (acc.) dark night (4) keeps away from pleasant home.

II

In a straight path guide my feet; not too (2) distant fields does my mind prompt (me) to view, (3) (being) too headstrong: one (4) step will now be enough for me.

III

Formerly I sought Thee not by prayers (as) a guide; (2) nor am I such-as I was, when alone (my) paths (3) to search-out I wished, (4) soon resolute to set-foot (on them).

IV

For the too-glittering day delighted (2) me, swelling with pride, nor yet unacquainted with (3) care: do Thou, I pray, of the age (4) gone-by be not mindful.

V

So through crags, wastes, torrents, *lead* me, (2) preserved so often by Thy power, (3) until, night being put to flight, (4) the rosy dawn grow light,

VI

and the long-lost company of loving ones (2) come forth

amid the ranks of the angels, (3) and, greeting with ardent (4) countenance the new-comer, rejoice.

HINTS

I. (1) "Omen," *auspex*; (4) "keeps away:" comp. Hor. *Od.* iv. 5. 12, "dulci distinct a domo."
II. (2) "Prompt:" comp. "In nova *fert animus*," etc., Ov. *Met.* i. 1.; (3) "too headstrong," *inportunior*, agr. with *animus*.
III. (4) "Resolute to," *pertinax* with inf. Comp. Hor. *Od.* iii. 29. 50, "ludum insolentem ludere pertinax."
IV. (2) "Pride," *fastus*; "unacquainted with," *inscius* (with gen.)
V. (1) "Wastes," *avia*, lit. "pathless places;" "torrent," *gurges*; (4) "dawn," *iubar*.
VI. (2) "Angels," *caelicolae, -ûm*.

EXERCISE LXVI[1]

Why dost thou haste, O morn? From ocean's bed
    Too early hast thou sped.
Before thy rising, clearer from afar
    Shone o'er rough waves the star;
The star to whose bright power the sailor prays
    Amid the doubtful ways:
And sweeter, midst the dewy shadows heard,
    Piped in yon elm the bird.
Sweet sleep, methought, drew near mine eyes to greet,
    Perchance with dreams as sweet.
Is there no spell thy hurry to beguile,
    And stay thee yet awhile?

                                C. S.

---

[1] This and the next Exercise are in "Systema Pythiambicum prius." See the Introduction, p. xli.

Retranslation

I

Why hastenest thou, Aurora? too hurriedly (thine) ocean (2) couch hast thou left, goddess. (3) Far more brightly, before thy rising, (pl.) over *rough* waves (4) shone the star,

II

whose bright power *the sailor* in uncertainty prays-to, (2) wandering over his course. (3) More sweetly meanwhile beneath the shades dripping with dew (4) did the denizen of the elm-tree sing.

III

And now, about to touch my eyes, kindly repose was at hand, with kindly (2) dreams perchance laden. (3) Whence am I to seek *a charm*, wherewith I *may persuade* thee, goddess, (though) hastening, to delay (4) a little while?

Hints

I. (1) "Hurriedly," *festina* (adj.); "ocean," *marinus*; (3) "more brightly," *splendentius*; "over" (sign of abl.); (4) "shone:" comp. Hor. *Od.* i. 12. 28, "simul alba nautis stella refulsit."

II. (1) "In uncertainty," *incertus*; (2) "wandering over," *oberrans*; "sailor," use the longer form, *navita*; (4) "denizen," *incola*.

III. (1) "Kindly," *almus*; (3) "am I to" (delib. subj.); "a charm," *ars* (abl., by attraction to the case of the relative); (4) "persuade," *suadeo*, with inf., as in Verg. *Aen.* xii. 814, "Iuturnam misero . . . succurrere fratri suasi."

EXERCISE LXVII

"A weary lot is thine, fair maid,
    A weary lot is thine!
To pull the thorn thy brow to braid,
    And press the rue for wine.
A lightsome eye, a soldier's mien,
    A feather of the blue,
A doublet of the Lincoln green—
    No more of me you knew,
        My love!
No more of me you knew!

"This morn is merry June, I trow,
    The rose is budding fain;
But she shall bloom in winter snow
    Ere we too meet again."
He turn'd his charger as he spake
    Upon the river shore;
He gave his bridle-reins a shake,
    Said "Adieu for evermore,
        My love!
And adieu for evermore!"

                      SCOTT.

RETRANSLATION

I

"The gods to thee, fairest maiden, an anxious lot (acc.), (2) a mournful lot, have given; (3) since thou, when about to bind thy brows with the rose, bindest them only with thorns; (4) and pressest the rue, not the cluster.

II

"How the eyes of thy swain glowed, and how he went in arms, (2) adorned with sky-blue crest; (3) and how, girt in doublet of green, he traversed the wood, (4) thou knewest; but, beyond this, nothing.

III

"'Tis morn, and, as the summer brings back her midmost warmth, (2) the flower of the rose delights to expand. (3) But that flower will blush in the winter snows before (4) that I returning shall have beheld thee."

IV

He ceased: and turning away while he cries Farewell! the reins (acc.) (1) he bent aside from the river's bank, (3) and shaking his bridle added these words at parting: (4) "My love! for ever farewell!"

HINTS

I. (1) "Anxious," *sollicitus*; (2) "mournful," *flebilis*: comp. Hor. *Od.* iii. 7. 1; (3) "since thou," *quae*, with subj.; "when about to" (fut. particip.); "only," *modo*; (4) "rue," *ruta*. If this should be thought too modern a way of expressing the idea, try "and pressest" (or "gatherest") "Sardinian *sardöus* herbs." Comp. Verg. *Ecl.* vii. 41, "Immo ego Sardois videar tibi amarior herbis;" where, however, the best MSS. have *Sardoniis*.

II. (1) "Swain," *puer*; (3) "doublet," *amictus*; (4) "knewest" (syncop. pluperf.)

III. (1) "As . . . brings back" (abl. absol.); "midmost," *medius*; (2) "expand," *turgeo*; (3) begin with *sed prius*; (4) "returning," *redux*.

IV. (1) "He ceased:" comp. Verg. *Aen.* ii. 152, *et passim*; (2) "bend aside," *retorqueo*: comp. Hor. *Od.* i. 2. 13; (3) "bridle," *frenum* (pl.); "at parting," *supremo ore*; (4) "my love," *lux nostra*.

EXERCISE LXVIII[1]

Break, break, break,
    On thy cold gray stones, O Sea!
And I would that my tongue could utter
    The thoughts that arise in me.

O well for the fisherman's boy,
    That he shouts with his sister at play!
O well for the sailor lad,
    That he sings in his boat on the bay!

And the stately ships go on
    To their haven under the hill;
But O for the touch of a vanish'd hand,
    And the sound of a voice that is still!

Break, break, break,
    At the foot of thy crags, O Sea!
But the tender grace of a day that is dead
    Will never come back to me.

                    TENNYSON.

RETRANSLATION

I

Dash on the rocks thy waters, surging sea, (2) whose shore is cold and chill: (3) my voice obstructed refuses to utter the complaints (4) which rise in my mind.

[1] This and the next Exercise are in "Systema Iambicum." See the Introduction, p. xlii.

II

Happy (is) you seafaring boy, *whom* it delights (2) with his sister to sport; (3) or (he) who, sitting in his hollow boat, his ditty (acc.) (4) renews free from care.

III

The ship with proud onset furrows the briny sea, (2) making for the hollow of the harbour: (3) who is to give to me the voices and the hands (4) which oblivion buries?

IV

Dash on the rocks thy water, surging sea, (2) over which a flinty crag is hanging: (3) alas! that the sweet grace of time that is past (4) refuses to return to me.

HINTS

I. (1) "Dash," *inlido* (with dat.); "surging," *aestuans*; (2) "is cold and chill," *alget frigidum*; (3) "obstructed," *impeditus*.

II. (1) "Happy (is):" comp. Hor. *Epod.* ii. 1, "Beatus ille qui procul negotiis;" "seafaring," *nauticus*; (3) "ditty," *cantilena*; (4) "free from," *solutus* (with gen.) Comp. Hor. *Od.* iii. 17. 16, "cum famulis operum solutis."

III. (1) "Onset," *impetus*; "briny sea," *salum*; (2) "making for," *appetens*; (3) "is to give" (delib. subj.); (4) "oblivion," *oblivium* (pl.); "bury," *comprimo*.

IV. (2) "Flinty," *durus*; "grace," *decor*; "that is past," *actus*; (4) "refuse," *denego*.

EXERCISE LXIX

GRACE FOR A CHILD

Here a little child I stand,
Heaving up my either hand:
Cold as paddocks though they be,
Here I lift them up to Thee;
For a benison to fall
On our meat, and on us all.
      Amen.
        HERRICK.

RETRANSLATION

Here Thou seest me stand before Thee, a tender child
Uplifting both hands:
(My hands) duly washed are like paddocks in coldness;
But I uplift both to Thee,
And pray (that) now in mercy this dinner (acc.), O God,
And each one dining, Thou wouldst bless.

HINTS

(1) "A tender child," *tenellus*; (2) "both," *uterque*; (3) "are like," "match," *aequo* (with acc.); "paddocks" (toads), *bufones*; (5) "in mercy," *benignus*; (6) "bless," *beo*.

EXERCISE LXX[1]

Three flies a-flying
Little thought they of dying:
One flew upon a piece of bread;
Feeding on alum, she dropped down quite dead.

---

[1] This Exercise is in continuous Iambics, the metre of the last Epode (the only example of it in Horace). See the Introduction, p. xliv.

Likewise the second
On sugary feast had reckon'd;
But for a speedy death was fated,
Because the sugar was adulterated.

From her small head
What tears the third did shed!
Quoth she, "Fly-paper on the wall
Will rid me soon from sorrow's lonely thrall."

Felo de se
In vain she wished to be:
How so? A third adulteration
Prevented death's much longed-for consummation.

J. G. L.

RETRANSLATION

Three flies were flying in fine weather:
Carelessly they enjoy the breeze, without thought of death.
But when one of them had tasted a piece of bread,
That, being adulterated, straightway killed the little one.
A sweet cake the second longed for;   5
But the drugged slice consigned her to a like death.
Streams (acc.) from her little eye did the third fly pour,
Mourning for her companions. "On the spot," she cries,
  "will I die."
And so she flies on to (some) paper attached to the wall,
Which boasts of being deadly to flies,   10
Detesting (her) life; but alas! unhappily surviving,
She finds the threats of promised death (to be) vain.

Hints

(1) "In fine weather," *sereno tempore;* (2) "carelessly," *temere* (the final *ĕ* is scanned short in early and late Latin, as in Plautus and Seneca; in the Augustan poets always elided); "without thought of," *securus* (with gen.); (3) "but when one of them," *quarum una . . . ut;* "piece," *crustum;* (4) "being adulterated," *corruptus:* "comp. Verg. *Georg.* ii. 466, "nec casia liquidi corrumpitur usus olivi;" "little one," *parvula;* (5) "cake," *placenta;* "long for," *concupisco;* (6) "drugged," "adulterated," *vitiatus;* "slice," *quadra:* comp. Mart. *Ep.* vi. 75. 1, "cum mittis turdumve mihi quadramve placentae;" (7) "little eye," *ocellus* (on the use of diminutives in Horace, see Pref., p. 10); (8) "on the spot," *ilico;* (9) "wall" (of a house), *paries;* (10) "of being" (inf.); "deadly," *mortifer;* (11) "unhappily," *male;* (12) "vain," *inanis.*

VOCABULARY

(To Exercises I.-XX.)

%.% *This Vocabulary is not meant to supersede the use of a Dictionary, but only to be a guide for the words to be used, so far as they are not already given in the Notes.*

Able, to be, possum
Adorn, to, dĕcŏro, orno, -āre
Affair, res
Affection, amor, studium
Again, iterum, rursus
Aged, senilis
Air, aura; (= the upper air), aethĕr, (= the lower), āĕr, -ĕris
Alas! heu, eheu (allowed as a spondee in Hor. Od. iii. 2. 9)
Alike, simul, pariter
All, omnis; all together, cunctus
Allowed, it is, licet
Alone (adj.) solus; (adv.) tantum
Along with, cum
Altar, ara
Amid, among, per, inter
Another (of two), alter
Any, ullus
Approach to, adeo, accedo, -ĕre
Arm, to, armo, -āre
Arms, arma, tela (n. pl.)
Arouse, to, suscito, excito, -āre
Arrow, sagitta

As, ut, ceu, velut, sicut, non secus ac
Ashamed, I am, pŭdet (me)
Ask, to, rŏgo, -āre; quaero, -ĕre
At least, saltem
At length, tandem, iam
Attendant, cŏmes, -ĭtis
Awake, to (transit.) cieo

Bad, mălus; badly, mălĕ
Bank, ripa
Bark (= ship), rătis
Barren, stĕrilis
Beauty, venustas
Bee, ăpis
Beguile, to, fallo, -ĕre
Behind, pŏnĕ (acc.)
Beloved, amatus, dilectus
Beneath, sub (abl.)
Benign, benignus
Beyond, ultra (acc.); (= more than), prae (abl.)
Bird, ăvis, volŭcer, ales, -ĭtis
Black, āter; (= glossy black), nĭger

Blast, flāmen, -ĭnis, flabrum
Blood, sanguis, cruor; bloody, cruentus
Bloom (= flourish), to, vireo
Boat, cumba
Bone, ŏs (ossis)
Bosom, gremium
Both (together), ambo
Bow, arcus; bowstring, nervus
Breath, spiritus, anima
Bride, nupta, sponsa
Bring, fĕro (ferre); bring back, refero
Brother, frāter
Bubble, to, scăteo
Buried, sepultus
But, sed, at (*ast* not used in the Odes); (= only), mŏdŏ
By (= at), ad

Call, to, voco, -āre
Care, cura; to care, curo, -āre; to take care (= beware), căveo
Cave, spĕcus, caverna
Celebrate, to, celebro, -āre
Chase, to, fugo, -āre
Cheek, gĕna
Child, puer, natus
Childhood, puertia; childlike, puerilis
City, urbs
Claim, to, vindico, -āre
Clear, clarus
Cloud, nubes
Colour, color, -ōris
Come, to, venio
Commotion (= din), strepitus
Companion, cŏmĕs, -ĭtis, socius
Complaint, questus, querella
Concealed, caecus

Conquor, to, vinco, -ĕre
Couch, lectus
Countenance, voltus, facies
Country, rus; (native), patria
Cover, to, condo, -ĕre
Cross, to, transeo, -ire
Crown (= chaplet), corona
Cruel, saevus, crudelis
Cry (aloud), to, clāmo, -āre

Daughter, filia
Day, dies; daily, diurnus
Daylight, lux (lūcis)
Dear, carus
Death, mors, fatum, letum; sometimes the inf. mŏri
Deem, to, crēdo, -ĕre
Defend, to, tueor
Delude, to, ludo, -ĕre
Deny, to, nĕgo, -āre
Depart, to, abeo, -ire
Despise, to, sperno, -ĕre
Destined, destĭnatus
Devoid, to be, careo (abl.)
Die, to, mŏrior (mori)
Displease, to, displiceo (dat.)
Disposition, indŏles
Distant, remotus, longinquus
Diverse, diversus
Door, fŏris (usu. in pl.); iānua
Draw, to, dūco, -ĕre
Dream, somnium
Drink, to, bĭbo, -ĕre
Drive, to, ago; drive away, abigo
Drop, gutta
Drum, tympănum
Dry, siccus; to dry up, sicco, -āre
Duly, rĭtĕ
Dutifulness, pietas
Dwell in, to, cŏlo, -ĕre (acc.)

Each, quisque, uterque
Ear, auris
Early, priscus, primus
Earth, terra, tellus, -ūris
Ease, to, lĕvo, -āre
Eastern, ēōus
Enough, săt, sătĭs
Enter, to, ineo, intro, -āre
Entreaty. *See* Prayer
Eulogy, laus
Even, vel, etiam
Ever, umquam ; (= always), semper, usque
Everywhere, passim, ubique
Evil (adj.) mălus ; (subst.), mălum
Exulting, laetus, exsultans
Eye, oculus, lumen

Face, ōs (ōris), facies, voltus
Fair, pulcher, candidus
Faith, fĭdes ; **faithful**, fĭdelis, fĭdus
Fall, to, căilo, -ĕre
Far, far off, prŏcul, longē
Farewell, valē, valeas
Farthest, extremus
Fate, fatum
Father, păter, genitor
Favour, to, faveo (dat.)
Festive, festus
Field, ăger, arvum
Fill, to, impleo, compleo, repleo
Fire, ignis ; **fiery**, igneus
Flame, flamma, ignis
Flashing, coruscus
Flatterer, fautor
Flight (of a bird), volatus
Flower, flōs ; **flowery**, floreus, floridus

Fly (= flee), to, fŭgio, -ĕre ; to fly as a bird, vŏlo, -āre
Follow, to, sequor (sequi)
Foot, footstep, pĕs (pĕdis)
For, nam, enim
Forbid, to, vĕto, -āre ; prohibeo
Form, forma, figura
Fount, fountain, fons
Free, liber ; **freedom**, libertas
Full, plenus

Garland, corona
Gentle, lēnis, tener, gĕnialis
Gift, dōnum, mūnus, -ĕris
Give, to, do (dăre)
Gladness, gaudium
Glide, to, lābor (labi)
Gloomy, tristis
Glory, gloria, laus
Glow, to, fulgeo, ardeo
Go, to, eo (īre)
God, deus, divus ; **goddess**, dea, diva
Gold, aurum ; **golden**, aureus
Grace, grātia
Great, magnus, ingens
Green, viridis ; **to be green**, vĭreo ; **to grow green**, vĭresco
Grief, dŏlor, luctus
Grot, antrum
Ground, hŭmus, sŏlum
Guard, to, tueor
Guardian, custos, -ōdis
Gushing, obortus

Hair, capillus
Hall, atrium, aula
Hard, durus
Harmful, noxius
Hasten, to, propero, -āre

Haughty, superbus, saevus
Head, caput, -itis
Hear, to, audio
Heart, cŏr, pectus, -ŏris
Height (mountain), iŭgum
Here, hic
Hid, to lie, lăteo
Hill, collis
Hind, dama
Hither, hūc
Hitherto, ante, antea, anthac
Hold, to, teneo
Hollow, căvus
Holy, sanctus
Hoof, ungula
Hope, spes
Horn, cornu
Hour, hora
How many, quot
How much, quantus
However (= yet), tamen
Hum, murmur, -ŭris
Human, humanus
Hurry, to, răpio, -ĕre
Husband, maritus, coniux, -ŭgis
Hymn, hymnus

Ill (with pain), aeger
Infant, infans (in the Augustan poets usu. an adj.; but subst. in Verg. *Aen.* vi. 427, Hor. *Od.* iii. 4. 20)
Infatuated, demens
Inferior, to be, cēdo, -ĕre (dat.)
Innumerable, numero carens, innumerus, innumerabilis
Instead of, pro (abl.)

Jest, to, iocor, -āri
Join, to, iungo, -ĕre

Joy, laetitia; joyful, laetus

Keep back (= delay), tardo, -āre
Kindly, bonus, benignus
King, rex
Know, to, scio, nōvi
Known, nōtus

Land, terra, tellus, -ūris
Laugh, risus; to laugh, rideo
Law, lex (lēgis)
Lay, to, pono, -ĕre; **lay aside**, depono
Lead, to, dūco, -ĕre
Leafy, frondens, frondosus
Leave, to, relinquo, -ĕre; linquo (no supine)
Length, at, tandem
Lest, nē
Lie, to, iăceo; **lie open**, păteo.
Life, vita, anima
Lift up, to, adtollo, -ĕre
Light, lux (lūcis), lūmen, -ĭnis
Light (adj.) lĕvis; lightly, lĕviter
Like, pār (păris), similis
Like as, ceu, velut, ac velut (but see the v. l. in Catull. lxviii. 65)
Live, to, vivo, -ĕre
Lo! ēn, ecce, adspice
Lofty, celsus, altus
Long (= for a long time), diu; no longer, non iam
Loss, damnum
Lot, sors
Lowly, humilis
Lurk, to, lăteo, latito, -āre
Lute, lyre, cithara, lyra, testudo, chĕlys, barbitŏs

Maiden, puella, virgo, -ĭnis

Manage, to, gero, -ĕre
Margin, margent, margo, -ĭnis
Mark, signum, nŏta; to mark, signo, -āre
Martial, martius
Mead, meadow, prātum
Merry, hilăris
Mind, mens, animus
Mindful, memŏr
Mist, nĕbŭla
Moist, ūvidus; moisture, ūmor
Month, mensis
Moon, luna
Morn, at, mānĕ
Mortal, mortalis
Moss, muscus; mossy, muscosus
Mother, māter, genetrix
Mound, tumulus
Mountain, mons
Movement, motus

Naiad, Naiăs, -ădis
Natal, natalis
Native, paternus
Naught, nil, nĭhĭl
Near, prŏpĕ (acc.)
Nest, nidus
Never, numquam, non umquam
New, novus; (= fresh), rĕcens
Night, nox; nightly, nocturnus
None, nemo; (adj.) nullus
Nourish, to, nūtrio
Now, nunc; (= by this time), iam
Nowhere, nusquam
Nymph, nympha, puella

Obscure, obscurus
Oft, often, saepe; as often, totiens; as often as, quotiens

Old, vetus, -ĕris, antiquus
Once (= once upon a time), quondam; (= once for all), sĕmĕl
Open, to be, pateo.
Or, vel; or else, aut
Orbit, orbis
Ornament, dĕcus, -ŏris
Over, per, super
Overcome, to, vinco, -ĕre, supero, -āre
Overshadow, umbro, obumbro, -āre

Pain, dŏlor; to be in pain, dŏleo
Pair, pār (păris)
Pan, Pan (gen. Pānis, acc. Pāna or Pānem)
Pass (time), to, duco, -ĕre; ăgo, -ĕre
Peace, pax (pācis)
Pelias, Pĕlias (gen. Peliae)
People, pŏpulus
Perchance, forsan, forsitan (subj.), fors
Pious (= dutiful), pius
Place, lŏcus; in place of, pro (abl.)
Plain, campus
Play, to, lūdo, -ĕre
Pleasure, voluptas; to be a pleasure to, placeo (dat.)
Plough, to, ăro, -āre
Ploughman, ărator
Plume, pinna
Poet, vātes
Pour, to, fundo, -ĕre
Praise, laus; to praise, laudo, -āre

Prayer, prex (nom. and gen. sing. not used; dat. and acc. sing. ante-class.; mostly in plural)
Present, to be, adsum
Press (press out), **to**, prĕmo, -ĕre
Prevail, to, văleo
Prey, praeda
Profane, prŏfanus
Proud, superbus
Pure, pūrus
Purple, purpŭra; (adj.) purpureus
Pursue, to, sequor (sequi)

Quick, cĕler, ălăcer
Quickly, cito

Rain, plŭvia; **rainy**, pluvius
Rapid, cĕler, vēlox, rapidus
Rare, rarus
Realm, regnum
Recall (= resemble), refero
Recess, recessus, latebrae
Redouble, to, itero, -āre, gemino (ingemino), -āre
Re-echo, to, resono; (trans.) reddo, -ĕre
Reed, calamus
Rehearse, to, itero, -āre
Rein, frēnum
Rejoice, to, gaudeo, laetor, -āri
Relate, to, refero
Remedy, medicamen, -ĭnis, medicina
Repair to, pĕto, -ĕre
Rest, quies, -ētis, requies; **to rest**, requiesco
Rest, the (= the others), reliqui, ceteri
Restless, inquietus, trepidus

Retreat, to, cēdo, -ĕre
Return, to (trans.) reddo; (intrans.) redeo, -ire
Revisit, reviso, -ĕre
Revolve (intrans.) **to**, volvor
Rich, dives, -ĭtis, opulentus
Right (subst.) ius (iūris); **rightly** (= correctly), recte; (= justly), iūrĕ
Rise, to, surgo, -ĕre, orior (oriri); (of a storm, etc.), ingruo
River, amnis, flūmen, flŭvius
Roam, to, văgor, -āri
Roof, tectum
Rose, rŏsa
Ruddy, rŭber; **ruddiness**, rŭbor
Rue (subst.) rūta
Rule, to, rĕgo

Sad (in sadness), tristis, aeger
Sail, vēlum
Scare, to, terreo
Sea, mărĕ, pontus, aequor, marmor; (open sea) pelagus; (adj.) marinus
Secluded, āmotus, occultus
Secret, sēcrētus
See, to, video
Seeing that, cum (subj.)
Self, ipse
Separate, to, sēpăro, disiungo
Serene, sĕrēnus
Settled, certus
Shade, umbra; **the shades** (disembodied spirits), animae, mānes
Shady, umbrosus
Shine, to, splendeo, fulgeo, nĭteo, renideo, corusco
Shore, litus, -ŏris, ōra
Shower, imber

Shut up, to, claudo, -ĕre
Sick, aeger
Sides, on all, undique, passim
Silent, sĭlens, tacitus
Silver, argentum ; silvery, argenteus
Sing, to, căno, -ĕre
Single, unus ; singly (use adj.)
Sister, sŏror
Sit, to, sĕdeo
Sky, caelum, pŏlus, aethēr, -ĕris
Slay, to, occīdo, -ĕre
Sleep, somnus ; deep sleep, sŏpor
Sleep, to, dormio
Smile, to, rideo, subrideo
Snow, nix (nĭvis)
So, sīc
Soldier, mīles, -itis
Song, cantus, carmen, -ĭnis
Soon, mox, brĕvi
Sound, sŏnus, sonitus, strepitus
Southern, australis
Spare, to, parco, -ĕre (dat.), (= to forbear), with inf.
Speak, loquor ; speak out, eloquor, profari
Specially, ūnĭcē
Sport, lūdus ; to sport, lūdo, -ĕre
Spouse, coniux, -ŭgis
Spread, to, sterno, -ĕre
Spring (of water), fons ; (of the year), vēr
Stain, măcula
Star, stella, sidus, astrum
Step, gressus, passus
Storm, procella, tempestas
Strain (= song), cantus ; (= din), strepitus
Stream, amnis ; *sometimes* unda

Strive, to, cōnor, -āri
Struck, pulsus
Struggle, to, luctor, -āri
Styx, the, Styx (Stўgis) ; Stygian, Stўgius
Such as, qualis
Sudden, on a, rĕpentē
Suitor, prŏcus
Summer, aestas, -ātis ; of summer, aestivus
Summit of, summus (agr. with noun)
Sun, sōl ; sunny, apricus
Surrender, to, trado, -ĕre
Surround, to, cingo, -ĕre
Suspect, to, suspicor, -āri
Sweet, dulcis, suavis
Swell, to (intrans.) turgeo
Swift, cĕler, vēlox

Take away, to, aufero, adimo, -ĕre
Take care (= beware), to, căveo
Tear, lacrima
Tell, to, dico, -ĕre
That (dem. pr.) ille ; (conj.) ut ; (= but that), quominus, quin
Then, tunc, tum ; (= next in order), dein, deinde
Thine, tuus
Thither, illuc
Thorn, spina
Thrice, ter
Throat, guttur, -ŭris
Thunder, tonitrus ; to thunder, tŏno, -āre
Time, tempus, -ŏris, aetas ; at times, quondam ; at the same time, simul ; 'tis time to, tempus (est), with inf.

Tongue, lingua
Too (too much), nĭmis, nimium
Touch, tactus
Trample, to, calco, -āre
Treasure, gaza
Triumph, triumphus
True, vērus; the truth, verum; Truth (personif.), Veritas
Trumpet, tŭba, classicum
Turf, cespes, -ĭtis
Turmoil, tumultus
Tyrant, tўrannus

Unerring, certus
United, iunctus
Upper, supĕrus
Utter, to, ĕdo, -ĕre, fundo, -ĕre

Vacant, vacuus
Vale (valley), vallis
Vapour, văpor
Victorious, victor (masc.) victrix (fem., admitting neut. pl.)
Vigour, vis (no gen. or dat. sing.)
Violet, vĭola
Voice, vox
Vow, votum; to vow, vŏveo

Wan, pallens, pallidus
Wander, to, erro, -āre, vagor, -āri
War, bellum
Water, aqua, lympha (sometimes unda); watery, ūdus
Wave, fluctus, unda
Waving, coruscus
Weariness, taedium
Weary, fessus, languidus
Weighty, grăvis
When (rel.) cum; (inter.), quando

Whence, unde
Where (rel.) qua, ubi; (inter.) ubi
While, dum (indic.)
Whirl, to, torqueo; (intrans.) torqueor
Whisper, sŭsurrus; to whisper, susurro, -āre
Whistle, sibilus; to whistle, strideo
Whoever, si quis, quisquis
Wife, uxor, coniux
Willing, vŏlens
Wind, ventus. (It is often preferable to use the name of some special wind, as Nŏtus, Auster, Eurus, etc.)
Window, fĕnestra
Wing, ala, pinna; winged, āles, -ĭtis
Winter, hiemps (hiemis)
Wish, to, vŏlo (velle)
Without, sine
Wood, silva, nĕmus, -ŏris
World, orbis; (= universe), mundus
Would that! utinam, o si (subj.)

Year, annus; yearly, annuus
Yesterday, hĕri, hesterno die; yesternight, hesterna nocte
Yet (= nevertheless), tamen; as yet, adhuc; not yet, nondum
Yield (afford), praebeo
Youth (season of), iuventus, -ūtis inventa
Youthful, iuvenis, iuvenilis

Zephyr, Zĕphўrus

INDEX OF FIRST LINES

	PAGE
A weary lot is thine, fair maid	17
Ah! si vous saviez comme on pleure	12
April made me: winter laid me here away asleep	90
Ask me no more: the moon may draw the sea	15
Avenge, O Lord, thy slaughter'd saints, whose bones	97
Break, break, break	115
Come, sweet harp, resounding	50
Cyriack, whose grandsire on the royal bench	69
Fair ship, that from the Italian shore	101
Fairest isle, all isles excelling	42
Fairy Queen! Fairy Queen!	23
From the forests and highlands	54
Go rouse the deer with horn and hound	25
Go up and watch the new-born rill	57
Here a little child I stand	117
Here sleeps my babe in silence	4
I held Love's head while it did ache	11
If thou wouldst find what holiest men have sought	74
In former days when, confined	39
In painted plumes superbly drest	45

King of kings and Lord of lords . .
Know ye not that lovely river? . . .

Last night, above the whistling wind . .
Lead, kindly light, amid the encircling gloom .
Like an army defeated . . . .
Loving she is, and tractable, though wild .

My Father's hope! my childhood's dream! .
My heart is disquieted within me . .
My youth is passing from me: in life's May .

No war, or battle's sound . . .

O bliss, when, all in circle drawn . .
Ὦ Ἡελίου θύγατερ . . . .
O thou who, exulting in golden youth . .

Play, Phœbus, on thy lute . . .

She dwelt among the untrodden ways . .
Soothed with the sound, the king grew vain .
Sweet Echo, sweetest nymph, that liv'st unseen
Sweet is the song of rivulets descending .

Tell me, thou star, whose wings of light .
That there's a self, which after death shall live
The heart of childhood is all mirth . .
The misty clouds, that fall sometime . .
The praise of Bacchus then the sweet musician sung
The rose had been washed, just washed in a shower
The world's great age begins anew . .
Therefore, sharers of my sufferings . .
Though the torrents from their fountains .
Three flies a-flying . . . .

	PAGE
Under the greenwood tree	1
Up to our altars, then	27
Welcome, welcome with one voice!	65
What ailed thee, Robin, that thou couldst pursue	5
When I survey the bright	76
When Nature tries her finest touch	86
While fates permit us, let's be merry	8
Whom we see not we revere	82
Why dost thou haste, O morn? From ocean's bed	111
You first I call on, brothers o'er the sea	62

THE END

Printed by R. & R. CLARK, *Edinburgh.*

www.ingramcontent.com/pod-product-compliance
Lightning Source LLC
Chambersburg PA
CBHW020252170426
43202CB00008B/342